AF248775

Scene in Sussex

ISBN 0 7050 0015 X
*Printed in Gt. Britain for The Research Publishing Co.
(Fudge & Co.,) London.*

Photograph: Richard

The River Cuckmere winding down to the sea at Cuckmere Haven

Scene in Sussex

a fresh look at the county by

RALPH LEWIS

THE RESEARCH PUBLISHING CO.
52 LINCOLN'S INN FIELDS
LONDON

FOR MY FAMILY AND FRIENDS
who have given love, laughter and the warmth of sunlight

CONTENTS

ACKNOWLEDGMENTS

I am indebted to the following friends for their contributions to this book:

Jeanie and Stanley Anscombe for their care, concern and kindness during miles of motoring. And for the verse by Jeanie Anscombe.

Gina Daniels and Rosslyn Glassman of The Witch Ball, 48 Meeting House Lane, Brighton for their research and generosity in providing the engravings.

Norman Battershill for his encouragement and for the drawings in " Saints and Sinners " (by kind permission of The Arun Art Centre) and elsewhere.

Richard Pike and Mike Jackson for their photographs.

Prelude

The Sussex Downs, which run from the Hampshire hills until they fade on the edge of Beachy Head, divide the woods and fields from the coastline. Sussex isn't a very large county, but the scenery and types of buildings have amazing variety.

West Sussex is defined by the boats and cool waters of Chichester and Bosham Harbours which Canute, when he reigned in his palace in that area, failed to rule. Brittania, according to the song, was luckier. Eastwards, from Beachy Head, you'll find sheep and the lonely marshes of Pevensey. The jagged outline of the castle, like Yorick's jaw, is a reminder of the place where William the Conqueror landed. Rye and Winchelsea, once busy ports, are the eastern ghosts of the county where the mists of Romney Marsh veil the promises of Kent.

If you travel across Sussex from east to west, ignoring the major roads that run north to south, you can follow the line of the Downs and discover the peaceful meadows, the hammer-head lakes and the woods, where wildlife has not yet been eliminated by the invasion of motor-cars. In the woods, you can stop, look and listen. The worst sounds you might hear are the gipsies swearing when their hedgehog stew boils over.

You can derive great pleasure from a day in the country and visit the historic houses, castles and priories. In the houses you might find craftsman made furniture and works of art of historical interest acquired by families who gave thought to the future. The county has a rich heritage of art, architecture, gardens, famous people and folk-lore. History isn't a stale subject. We're making it now. But, like the two nuns who passed on each side of the drunkard and were greeted by: " How the heck did she do that?", you can be deluded by dull guide-books.

Any worthwhile outing is usually better planned in advance. The risk of making mistakes is lessened and the pleasure of the occasion might be increased. You don't have to load yourself like a pack-mule with a mountain of maps and tastefully

designed brochures to enjoy a day out. Only masochists have
to do that. There are certain people, I know, who treat every
outing or picnic as a challenge to hâute cuisine and hâute
couture. They probably end up eating a banquet in a bug-
infested dell with an adder on their apple charlotte. They may
even have to climb the dusty turrets of a fading family mansion
unacceptable to the National Trust where a Balenciaga outfit
won't beat back bats or check the chilly blast from the headless
lady in the West wing.

Whether you travel by bus, motor-car or Shank's pony do
make sure that the place you want to see is open to the public
on the day you have decided to visit it. You may prefer the
errors of enthusiasm to the indifference of wisdom but a quick
check with the local information office will confirm that the
fine old example of Victorian Ruritania is waiting, open gates,
to greet you. Most of the well-known Sussex country houses
are on accessible routes and are kept in splendid condition.
But there are a few off the beaten track standing on water-
logged ground in a state of genteel decay. In these, the hygiene
notices for visitors have been half nibbled away by either
wrath or rats.

Sussex is different from other counties because of the old
ways and customs that still survive today. Flint and chalk
have played a vital part in the life of the county. The coast has
increased in popularity with British and Continental visitors
during the past ten years. The bucket-and-spade brigade gets
bigger every summer and so does the litter through which we
have to stumble like pigs in paper clover. You may wish to
seek a peaceful haven of great beauty and find that everyone
else had the same idea on the same day. Some places that were
once a cherished memory of peace and quiet have become,
through new roads, a blaring nightmare of cars and chaos.
Some places have been ruined by land developers. These you
can recognise when they say to each other: " Pull up a tree and
sit down." The merchants of Venice, 500 years ago, were every
bit as greedy and grasping as developers are today. But at
least they built Venice. The moral would seem to be that you
can't leave footprints in the sands of time by sitting on your
bottom.

Francis Bacon said that " houses are built to live in and not
look on." This is arrant nonsense from the same man who said
that " hope is a good breakfast but a bad supper." The great
houses in our county, like Parham and the Priest's house — old
and humble — at Alfriston, were designed to suit the needs of
their owners and still give aesthetic pleasure to visitors. Their
architecture is distinctive. I don't know when we lost the

knack of building beautiful buildings but lose it — in wide terms — we certainly did. There are pleasant examples of fine 20th Century architecture usually standing in isolation.

Sussex is surprisingly rich in romantic architecture and scenery; houses that have gardens designed to compliment them, river and water meadows, castles and cathedrals, follies and grottoes. Strangely, many people assume that architecture and scenery just happen and that they are permanent. Don't you believe it! The sea erodes — look at Beachy Head and Seaford — and buildings decay through lack of interest and lack of money. Changes occur all the time, particularly in geological structure. Changing beauty is worth viewing and recording while it lasts.

Hilaire Belloc wrote about the chalk of Sussex: " Its lovely breadths delight us when the white clouds and the flocks move over them together; when the waves break into cliffs they are the characteristics of our shores and through its thin coat of whitish mould go the thirsty roots of our three trees, the beech, the holly and the yew."

Exploring the towns and countryside is one way of avoiding boredom, which can be fattening. For those who can't travel because of health or age, then reading and hearing about other people's experiences is a pleasant alternative to television. Travelling in Sussex is as refreshing, to me, as a summer holiday in the South of France. There, too, it is frequently cold and wet and deserves the nickname of the " Overcôte d'Azur." Whatever the weather in Sussex, you'll find a day out exploring is exceedingly good for your morale. Ask any woman whose morale has been boosted by a wink from a man.

1. Early Sussex. Skulls and Skullduggery

The name of Piltdown conjures up, for most people, an odd shaped skull and bearded diggers. It took a million years to make an overnight success and to raise the curiosity of ladies with moustaches, wearing elastic sided boots, in 1912.

The strange cocoanut shape that Charles Dawson offered the world as the fossil skull of Piltdown man saw the light of day in that year during a dig in Sussex. This was either a splendid hoax or a record of Dawn Man, creature of the Early Pleistocene period, when you didn't join clubs but swung them. Was he your forefather and mine, perhaps, a rather pathetic reminder of how we are able to speak and remember facts today? Personally, I prefer to see the event as a backward version of Darwin's theory — or how to make monkeys out of men.

The Palaeolithic world had many strange creatures which roamed the Sussex countryside, and the bones of them are still on view in the museum of the Sussex Archaeological Society. The River Ouse where the creatures gathered was, at the time of their existence, eighty feet higher that it is today. You can hear the early hunters saying, when their wives complained of seeing a horrible lump on the landscape: " Woman sick! "

Imagine carving the Sunday joint with a flint. That was the only tool that the Prehistoric people had to use when fingers failed. Their lamps were rough cups of hollowed chalk with a wick floating in grease from the meat which they cooked. The golden gorse that grows wild on Cissbury Ring today has overgrown and filled in shafts of the old flint mine, which was the most famous in the county. The other mines round Worthing, Chichester and Findon include Blackpath Hill, Harrow Hill, Bow Hill, Stoke Down, Tolmere Pond and Lavant Caves. But Cissbury Ring was the most famous and, within the chalk underground, the Neolithic miners dug for flints with picks made from the antlers of red deer. You can see the Seven Sisters beyond the mouth of the Cuckmere from the grass covered earthwork and rampart today, when only depressions in the ground show where the original mine-shafts were located. The Isle of Wight is visible to the West and the beech trees of Chanctonbury, which was bare in the Stone Age. In those days you couldn't have your mate and eat him.

Flint was knapped at Cissbury and this was one of the early forms of craftsmanship. The metal implements of the Bronze and Iron Age were the prerogative of the wealthy who valued them with the reverence that maiden aunts sometimes have for their silver heirlooms today. The majority of people had to be content with flint implements as the majority, today, have to be content with stainless steel. Flints had many purposes. Red hot flints were used to heat water into which they were dropped. They were used to seal raw meat in an age when hâute cuisine was primitive and packed with protein.

The Downs are still the place where evidence exists of people in the Neolithic and Bronze Ages. Burial mounds, long and round barrows and traces of early agricultural work mark out their existence in life and in death. Green porcelain amulets and beads of amber or jet were buried with the dead to be discovered when the earth yielded them up again. Broken axes, urns and beakers — decorated pots marked with finger-nail and cord — leave no doubt regarding the skill of the early potters through whose work, the remaining fragments, we can judge the extent of their civilisation and their cultures. The shaping of clay to produce ceramics has a timeless quality, an achievement which is almost indestructible.

Mount Caburn, near Lewes, is one of the early Downland forts with earthwork surrounding the head. These entrench-ments were achieved with limited implements, infinite patience and great skill. Those in Dorset and Wiltshire have a scale and grandeur that makes them distinctive landmarks. Caburn was once an island between the Ouse and Glynde Reach. In that period large areas of Sussex were under water; Steyning was a port and Winchelsea and Rye had waves pounding against their cliffs. The sea also covered Pevensey Level. But the Downs were always a dominant feature and inspired the early potters to shape and mould their pottery on lines suggested by nature. The red amber cup, of this age, found in Hove this century was a rare piece, surprisingly sophisticated for people who conducted their affairs in a language consisting of sighs and grunts.

Too many people have romanticised about Roman legionaries tramping to and from the 23 hill forts on the Downs. These forts and camps credited to the Romans prove to be of an earlier Neolithic origin. A similar wealth of legend haunts Stone-henge, which is extremely draughty. Strangely, there is an odd

Saxon Weaver's Hut at The Open Air Museum, Singleton
A reconstruction (c.500 AD) based on huts excavated at
Old Erringham and Bishopstone
(Reproduced by courtesy of John Lowe)

County Hall at Lewes
Offices designed for the East Sussex County Council by County Architect
Jack Catchpole and the Architect's Department.
(Reproduced by courtesy of Guy Gravett)

Aerial view of harvesting near Chichester

Demonstration of steam threshing at Goddards Green

tendency for amateur archaeologists to be vague about how long the Romans were with us.

In actual fact they were against us. Snobberies about their genius are quite engaging and help rather than harm. The Romans seldom covered their tracks despite their good army training. Warriors, before the Romans, were tall men who protected themselves with animal skins and used stone weapons to defend themselves. Some wore bronze plating, primitive but effective, and others wore helmets with the horned casque of the iron period. They ruled their watery kingdom until the Romans came. The Romans, when they did come, were short in stature, like their swords, and had shields emblazoned with lightning.

They never needed to strike in the same place twice.

2. Roman Sussex. Walls that had Ears

Life goes on for a surprisingly long time despite the exhausted words of those who complain about how quickly the years seem to go as they grow older. If you set out to do or achieve anything you are sure to become quite good at it with concentration and in time.

The Romans, though not fond of the sea and the tides in the English Channel, were good at absorbing new territories. Their excuse, if one was needed, for invading Britain was that our country must be subdued so that the ties of friendship with Rome could be strengthened. The year was 43 A.D. The Romans were born leaders and, as they tramped over Sussex after a quick march along the north shore of Kent and a bloody battle on the Medway, they found little or no resistance to their true plan of expansion. They were decisive, like good business-men, and did not meet competition. They crushed it when necessary. The Weald held no terrors for them and their influence spread across West Sussex — Stane Street, Bignor, Southwick, Angmering and Wiggonholt.

Today, the Roman Villa at Bignor, Pulborough is one of the largest in the country with a fine museum open to the public from March to October and every Sunday in November. But the most stunning masonry building in Roman style is at Fishbourne, too large for a house or a villa and therefore a palace of the period. The Roman palace was discovered in Spring, 1960, when a workman cut through Roman tiles while digging the trench for a water-main in a field north of the village. The local archaeology committee were informed and when the first trial excavation began in 1961 parts of the extensive building showed that the structure was earlier in origin than any other Roman dwelling in the British country-side. Timber buildings of an earlier period were also found below the foundations. These were storehouses and a workshop built between 43 and 75 A.D.

In 1961, six mosaic floors — including the finest depicting a boy on a dolphin in the centre — and the main masonry structure were uncovered and assessed as having been built between 70 and 80 A.D. By 1965 new mosaics were uncovered, together with the marble head of a boy (probably a member of the owner's family) and enough evidence to piece together the history of the palace and the lives of those who lived there. But one of the finest discoveries was the vast formal garden divided by an avenue 40 feet wide and containing the original bedding trenches. The Romans, according to evidence, liked roses and climbing plants as well as box hedge, acanthus, rue, rosemary and lilies. The garden also had marble basins and fountains fed by pipes. The layout was elaborate and could have made an elegant contribution to the Roman equivalent of *House and Garden*.

The beginnings of the Roman military site — the first two buildings excavated at Fishbourne were military in character — and the subsequent increase of civilian population, resulting in a palace fit for a king, caught the imagination of the public as well as the archaeologists at the time of the excavations. That interest increases each year and today Fishbourne is a major tourist attraction. There is evidence to suggest that the palace was destroyed by fire about 270 A.D. particularly when you consider that the thick covering of charcoal over the floors could have resulted from burnt rafters. Nobody knows how the fire started but there are two theories. One is that it might have been caused by an army of barbarians from Gaul who invaded the area and the other attributes the catastrophe to the actions of careless workmen. These were as numerous in Roman times as they are today.

When the palace was built, the colonnaded garden was surrounded by magnificent buildings with plastered and painted walls decorated by panels enclosing flowers, tendrils and fish brightly coloured. The floors were black and white, inlaid with coloured stones of various shapes. The owner could have been Cogidubnus, since the wealth of a king would have been justification for building a palace in masonry. His capital, as well as the source of his wealth, was Chichester one mile away from Fishbourne. The decision to excavate the palace for public exhibition cost more than £200,000 and the money was raised by various trusts and individuals to whom we owe thanks, that really neglected form of compensation.

A major contribution to Sussex was the building of roads by the Romans. These were a far cry from the cluttered chaos of motorways today when most drivers have forgotten how to walk. The Roman roads were functional and built for men to march along singing, I imagine, the usual type of sweet Army song. Stane Street was designed to run from Chichester to

London, curving in places which broke tradition with the Roman rule of straight lines for their roads. Mosaic pavements, where they have been unearthed, show that the builders had a preference for bland colours related to the natural origins of their materials which, probably, did not originate in Sussex. The mosaic stones were blue, green, red, brown and white and therefore could have been imported from Italy. The subject matter in most of the pavings unearthed suggest an Italian background which is logical when one remembers the influence of Rome. You don't expect roast beef from a cook used to spaghetti.

Villas, roads and amphitheatres are the main heritage left to us by the Romans who, unlike the Normans and Saxons, were never really at home in any country except their own despite the fact that they came, saw and conquered. But some had to stay as the Roman cemeteries prove, particularly the famous one at Hassocks. The cemeteries were built near the side of roads and one assumes that foot-slogging was not only hazardous but also lethal. In the graves there have been fine burial urns, bowls and coins perhaps put there by their owners as a reassurance of eternal life. Walter Gropius, the architect, had a light hearted view of death when he said: " The piety for cinders is a half-way thing. Out with it!"

Roman rule lasted almost four hundred years in Sussex, although people at the time might have remarked that it seemed longer. The rulers were military and, therefore, disciplinarians. Their justice was harsh and their planning of towns and roads was functional. Visit Chichester today and you'll see the original plan of intersecting roads and the Market Cross denoting the Roman market place. The roads in those times were metalled and the iron for them came from the eastern side of the county and Kent. Fields and gardens today cover the rusted surfaces of the Roman routes. They are as useless as our modern highways will be in another century.

The Western side of Sussex is milder than the Eastern side and therefore the discerning ex-patriates of Rome set up their centre in Chichester where the majority of villas were built. Some had central courts, built in the reign of Antonius, like the one at Bosham. There were baths and gardens as well as every civilised mod.con. that a Roman matron, keeping up with the Juniuses, could want. Roman busts were exceptionally impressive. The Council House tablet, in Chichester, was given by the Guild of Builders during the reign of Cogidubnus over his kingdom of Sussex as the start of a temple before the town became a cathedral city and converted to Christianity. The

Cathedral today covers Roman buildings and the walls of the city are Roman.

Cogidubnus, whose palace could have been the one at Fishbourne, was a Roman in his tastes and inclinations. The government, in his day, took care of their noblemen in exile and when, in 43 A.D., he landed in the Selsey-Fishbourne area he was not only supported by the Roman army but was assured of a royal reward. Vespasian, a gifted soldier later to become emperor, conquered the Isle of Wight, destroyed 20 fortified capitals and crushed tribes in Dorset and Somerset through the friendly help of Cogidubnus. The king allowed Vespasian the use of supply bases in Sussex, one of which could have been Fishbourne, then a port, at a time when the military were in occupation there as well as at Chichester.

The Roman walls surrounding Pevensey Castle, a Norman building complete with moat owned by the National Trust, once encircled ten acres of land. The walls, despite their sturdy appearance, were built on foundations that would never pass Building Regulations today. The gaunt remains of the work by Romans and Normans, the garrison's well and the high walls with bastions, overlooking the grass that has replaced the sea, are an impressive monument to a time when tribal Romans didn't inhabit towns, only counties. The Romans built durable walls swiftly and without anxiety, the occupational disease of architects today. Their walls are still visible above ground unlike so many of their villas and other buildings which either remain buried or were pillaged by Saxons.

Roads, too, have disappeared under fields and estates as well as coins, pottery and the marble busts which the Romans treasured. Their cats, which wandered and sunned themselves in the colonnaded courtyards, are buried bones like their owners. It is a strange fact that bricks, used for building, were not used again until hundreds of years after the Roman rule. Strange, too, that there was virtually no bloodshed and few outbreaks of civil disobedience under the conquerors, who disciplined the people of Sussex for 400 years. Some people today consider that our Roman history is a form of treasure.

In terms of personal freedom it is the sort of treasure that is better buried.

3. Saxon Sussex. Waltzing Queen Matilda

Lady Gundrada was the wife of the first Lord of Lewes after the conquest — William de Warenne. She was also the daughter of King William and Queen Matilda, who seized every occasion to pray when she was not preying on people. She was also a nifty dancer by Saxon ballroom standards if you believe legends. Even if you don't, it is fact that Christianity came to Sussex in the Saxon age.

The remains of Saxon influence in agriculture and decoration can be seen throughout the county. Fragments and features of Saxon building work can be found today in Sussex churches. The church at Bosham is recorded in the Bayeux Tapestry which shows Harold entering the building to receive the sacrament. The tower is Saxon, and, although Roman work is visible within the walls, the decoration and arched doorway are Saxon to the stone. The Saxons, despite their skill as stone masons, were gifted carpenters as their timber architecture shows. However, many of the cottages which they built were crude and roughly constructed. The best Saxon builders, all who didn't accept that the sky was the limit, were those who excelled in building churches.

Worth was once a forest, as the name implies, and today the great beeches and yews are all that remain to remind us of the fact. The church at Worth has large arches to distinguish it and small windows that suggest a siege was always imminent at the time when it was built. This is a unique piece of architecture like Sompting church, graced by a splendid four-sided tower which has been described as a " Rhenish helm " after the German and Rhenish Romanesque examples. St. Mary's is elegant in design, high and unbuttressed, and was probably built in the year 1,000 which was fifty years later than most of the Saxon buildings in Sussex. Sadly, the church is not enchanced by a swarm of bungalows and seedy trimmings of modern life which surround it.

St. Nicholas at Worth and St. Mary at Sompting are pure Saxon architecture, large in scale and bold in conception. They are unlike St. Andrew's, the church at Bishopstone, which lies in a hollow of the Downs close to the mouth of the Ouse. Bishopstone has a bit of everything, a mongrel building of historical pedigree. The building dates back to the eighth century. The doorway, with a round head but without mouldings, is probably Saxon like the sundial in the gable above. This south doorway is also distinguished by the fact that it is not in the centre. There are Norman additions and alterations and a bit of Early English, the ornate arches east and west of the chancel, thrown in for good measure. The existing rib vault dates about mid-nineteenth century and the chronology of the building is enough to baffle the most erudite historian. But the church adds a touch of beauty to the area of Newhaven, which is not noted for its contribution to English architecture. The port is a pleasant place, as most ports are, with people eternally poised in action like humming birds.

Bishopstone church is recorded in the Domesday Book, but there are a great many churches in Sussex with pieces of Saxon work as at Bosham. Saxon building was prolific throughout the county. You can see the features which distinguished it; square flint towers, some with coned lids, flint walls, porches with long and short work, arches plain, arches with dog-tooth moulding and tombstones with decorative carving. There were cemeteries at Alfriston and Worthing, foundations of houses that spread from Steyning to the northern edge of the county and numerous fragments in our churches. Judging from the extensive chipping, decorating and sawing that the average Saxon managed to do, he must have been remarkably free from rheumatism in his shoulders.

The forest areas in Saxon times had place names ending in hurst, den, lye and worth. You can spot them today in place names like Midhurst, Shipley, Iden and Petworth. The main Saxon name ending was ING which defined a meadow that must have existed at Ditchling, Beeding and Lancing among many. Tun, too, was popular since it defined an enclosure as at Singleton, Rustington and Chiltington. Fold, as in Cowfold, field, as in Mayfield and ham, as in Burpham, each reveal the Saxon beginnings. Borstal, a formidable word today, was used in Saxon times to describe an ascent up the Downs and pinpointed those villages which lay in the hollows. What's in a name? History, naturally, revealing that most men were born to be used. It's still true today, although some men and women in all centuries have had a spirit of independence and adventure that mark them as rare individuals.

Coins in Saxon times were minted at Steyning and also at Chichester, Hastings and Lewes, where there were two mints.

You can unearth those coins today, a single penny, and with luck, a hidden hoard. The penny bears the head of Harold, who looks sly even though he wears a crown and beard. His fate, at Hastings where he was killed by an arrow, was a confirmation of the Saxon belief that fear kept the elderly pure. The history of Normandy and Sussex has its fair share of blood and thunder and Harold's association with both Hastings and Bosham stimulates the tourist trade in those places today.

Romanticism in the 18th and 19th centuries was excessive and encouraged delusions as an antidote to harsh reality In the 20th century, we have made a sort of magic out of technology, a harsh reality, and subdued romanticism. History might repeat itself given time. There are echoes of the 'sixties of this century in the records of Saxon life. The Saxons loved bright colours, swinging clothes, brooches and beads. The women had beauty aids as early as the seventh century and in one of the fifteen graves opened in a Christian cemetery near Broadstairs, Kent there were pins, keys, tweezers and beads. Knives, spearheads, a bronze garter buckle and an iron belt were also found which suggest that honour in those days had to be defended. Even today you can see looks inherited from our Anglo-Saxon ancestors, blonde hair, blue eyes and tall figures. You will even hear the words which they used. In Ecclesiastes, chapter one, you will find a fitting comment:

> All the rivers run into the sea; yet the sea is not full . . .
> the eye is not satisfied with seeing, nor the ear filled with
> hearing . . .
> And there is no new thing under the sun.

I don't know whether King Alfred, a while before Harold, burnt cakes but he was certainly recorded as having lived in West Dean, near Eastbourne. Strangely, there are two West Deans and two East Deans in Sussex which causes visitors to the county a great deal of anguish when they make a mistake with directions. The Manor House in West Dean, near Eastbourne, could mark the spot where King Alfred had a palace at a time when the area was known as Dene and the language was called Sudsexe. The King's lands included the area of Ditchling known as Court Farm and also parts of Lullington and Sutton in addition to the palace. King Alfred was reputed to be kind and hospitable, generous and Christian. He must have realised that a loving heart is the beginning of all knowledge.

Sadly, in Saxon times, the best way to be safe was never to feel secure.

4. Saints and Sinners.
Gladly my cross-eyed Bear

You can't wear the same clothes everyday unless you're very rich or a saint. But the Saxons who were poor and pious had to make their cloth last. They relied on multi-coloured beads, buckles and brooches to adorn the plain material of their dress. It was an advanced concept of Unisex, since men and women enjoyed adornments of amber, rock crystal, black glass, coloured porcelain, bronze and silver. This was also a considerable advance on fashions of former years — the skins of the Stone Age and the armour of the Romans. The jewels were even taken to the grave where, in subsequent centuries, they have been unearthed to show the tastes of our ancestors.

When the Saxons died, they left for posterity their Christian architecture, agriculture and decoration throughout Sussex. Towers, churches, villages with meadows ringed with elms, farmyards, decorated stonework and other reminders of their masonry and agricultural skills. Although Christianity came late to Sussex, previously considered to be a heathen cut-off county, it brought a new Saxon descriptive word, Selig, meaning blessed. The word also meant holy, at a time when the conversion of the county was undertaken by St. Wilfred, who could be described as the earliest evangelist.

St. Wilfred was a handsome man, energetic and tireless when he travelled. He was Bishop of York until spite and envy in church circles there drove him south. He came to Sussex by accident on his first visit when he was ship-wrecked returning from Compiègne and escaped attack from the crowd waiting for the spoils of the sea. His second visit, in the year 680, was on his own decision at a time when there was famine and drought. There was a need for a miracle and when St. Wilfred prayed for rain, which came, he laid the foundation stone for the conversion of the heathens. His monastery was on Selesey, the seal island, near Bosham where a small colony of monks had existed previously. Although he only stayed in the county five years his achievements lasted through the centuries.

St. Cuthman was another Sussex saint — who some say was mythical — remembered for his work and the church he built on the fork of the river at Steyning. This is the place where he is reputed to be buried. He apparently led the simple life of a shepherd and pulled his old mother across the fields in a wheelbarrow when she was unable to walk. He did good works and when these took him from his flock of sheep he encircled them with his crook to ensure their safety. This legend is still believed today when herds of sheep bunch together at the approach of danger. It may, however, be simply explained by the fact that there is safety in numbers. He would have been a cheerful man, I imagine, whose life might have been a series of adventures in contentment among the fields and villages of rural Sussex.

St. Cuthman, in legend, is praised for defeating the Devil, who was hell-bent on digging a dyke that would let in the sea and flood the lowlands. The piety of the people had, understandably, reached a stage where drastic action was necessary. But the Saint, with his friend Sister Ursula, came to the rescue of his flock, hoodwinked the Devil with rustic cunning and saved Hove — as we know it today — from sinking into the sea. The Devil's Dyke remains a landmark, a popular haunt for courting couples who seem to prefer the devil they know.

The farmland of Devil's Dyke Farm, covering 346 acres, is leased from the Crown. Saddlescombe Farm nearby is

protected by the surrounding hills, where pit dwellings have been discovered, and the sites of British and Roman camps on the North Hill and the Dyke. Saddlescombe Manor, recorded in the Domesday Book, once had 13 acres of meadowland when it was owned by Geoffrey de Saye in 1225. In that year it became the Preceptory of the Knight Templars, powerful soldier monks, whose reputation caused the Pope to dissolve their order in the 14th century. Henry the Eighth seized the property during his reign and sold it to Sir Anthony Brown, then owner of Poynings Castle which adjoined the land. The Lords of the Manor of Saddlescombe, titled Viscounts Montecute, controlled the land for 200 years and were also Lords of Cowdray. Jousting then was only slightly more vicious than polo is today. Finally the Leconsfields took possession for three generations until the Robinson family, who succeeded them, sold the estate — 550 acres including farm-house, cottages and outbuildings — to the Brighton Corporation in 1926.

Democracy today enables everybody to decide who shall spend their money. There was very little democracy in Saxon times in Sussex and very little money for the average Christian. Murder, martyrdom and mayhem were as active as they are today. Men were dismembered, imprisoned, persecuted and exiled. The Saxon's Devil, delighted by the large number of idle hands and infuriated by the increasing number of churches, smote the Downs in an effort to drown the righteous. The saints and sinners of all ages have that indefinable quality that distinguishes them from the crowd. Certainly they are people with individual qualities that have the courage to be themselves, good or bad. Their actions are eccentric, some-times unbelievable and you know their quality. You can't see it. Such people have always broken the rules and can be recognised by their refusal to compromise. They have style.

St. Dunstan must have had style. He possessed a sense of humour and was a remarkable craftsman with the ability to cope with devils. He was a metalworker and his golden chalices could have graced the Goldsmith's Hall. "How splendid! " the Devil might have remarked as the flames in the smithy at Mayfield, where St. Dunstan worked, blazed. The tone of his voice, however, would have been at variance with the stoney look in his eyes. Legend doesn't have to be believed but, according to it, the Devil was given a nose-bob by St. Dunstan with a pair of red-hot tongs.

Nuns today would persuade you by faith rather than rely on legends and their convent at Mayfield was once the Palace of the Archbishops of Canterbury. A friend of mine, Sister Mary

Claire, used to say that nothing is impossible. She also used to add: "Miracles take a little longer." The name of St. Dunstan is associated with the blind, and the fine modern building by Sir John Burnett, Tait and Lorne, architects, dominates the high ground at Ovingdean. At the time that I completed my architectural thesis on building for the adult blind, the vibration of the potato peeler in the kitchen on the top floor could be clearly heard in the entrance hall on the ground floor. Blind people have a wonderful sense of humour, I've found, and when I mentioned that the position of St. Dunstan's was ideal since it faced the sea I received the reply: "Yes, and on a windy day you're in it!" This remark was capped by four blind friends of mine in a Rottingdean public house where the publican always reminded customers that there was a collecting box for the blind on the counter. My friends suggested that he emptied the contents to pay for their drinks and cut out the middle man. It would have appealed to St. Dunstan's sense of humour, I think.

William, Earl de Warenne, was a soldier and the Lord of Sussex. He built the Priory of St. Pancras at Lewes. The ruins today give no indication of its original beauty and, cruelly, time has left no shell to reveal the splendour and size of the building. If the building was a personal gesture to expiate the Earl's earlier sinning, what does it matter? Nobody is perfect except my grandfather, who always said *he* was. And too many tourists have pieces of sticking plaster on their Achilles tendons from trying to seek the reasons and secrets behind architecture which, in its time, served purely human needs. Anyway, the Priory of St. Pancras was built about the end of the 11th century after William de Warenne had decided to introduce the Cluniac reforms to England. William and his wife Gundrada had visited Rome and had also seen the abbey of Cluny in Burgundy. After their tour in 1075, the couple built the church at Southover for the Cluniac monks two years later. Today, the railway lines run over what was once the chapter house of the great Priory, although the corner of the refectory, the undercroft of the once vaulted dormitory and parts of the infirmary chapel, added a century later, still exist. You have to recreate history for yourself in the area and listen to the winds on the Downs where they sound like a pack of hounds in full cry.

Sussex, like the monks of the past, has been girdled in splendour by monasteries. The Carmelites were at Shoreham, the Dominicans at Arundel and the Benedictines at Boxgroves. These were among the thirty great centres which also included Chichester, Winchelsea, Michelbourne, Pynham and Rye.

There have been martyrs at Lewes, scene of many violent actions that are still remembered on Bonfire Night when the anti-Catholic cries of " No Popery! " echo back to a time when seventeen martyrs were burnt in Lewes in 1556. Bonfire Night is also associated with the destruction of Lewes Priory by Portinari, engineer to Henry the Eighth, who fired the wooden underpinning which he used to support the decaying walls.

The indifference and intolerance that destroyed lives and fine buildings like the Priory make you question whether hearts abloom with sin are not less dangerous than hearts gone yellow and dry?

As Sir Henry Channon remarked: " Reformers are always finally neglected, while the memoirs of the frivolous will always be eagerly read."

How true! At least when we're young we try to be faithful and are not. But when we're old we want to be and cannot. And this applies to both saints and sinners.

5. Glynde, Glyndebourne and Lewes. High Streets and Low Notes

Glyde is 4 miles south east of Lewes off the A.27 and Glyndebourne is 1 mile north of Glynde.

Old guide books and museum catalogues tended to suffer from foot and note disease. You don't need a guide book for the village of Glynde which is like a living museum covering 400 years of history. You'll find dignity and enjoyment in the old houses and their surroundings. Mount Caburn — one of the great ramparts of the Downs — overlooks the village and was used by our ancestors before the Romans ruled us. Superstitious folk say that you can hear the ghostly sound of men marching on this part of the Downs but I've listened and only heard the wind sighing as it stirs the wild grass that dresses the dips and hollows.

Some people know everything about architecture except how to enjoy it. There are three buildings in Glynde which should satisfy the most diverse tastes. The church of St. Mary is unlike any Parish Church I've ever seen. The style is classical (even Hussey in 1852 described the church as being " in a very bad taste, the style called Grecian ") and the dark formal atmosphere reminds one of a private chapel or a city church. The church was built in 1763 by Sir Thomas Robinson, an amateur Palladian, who left us a precise account of the labour costs and materials used in the building. The church is a record of people in addition to being an interesting piece of architecture. Windows record the memory of Lord Hampden, Speaker of the House of Commons for 12 years. Herbert Morley, who helped recapture Arundel and Chichester for Parliament, is also remembered.

Both these men lived in Glynde Place, a quadrangular house built for William Morley in the 16th century. The house is next door to the church and the grounds cover 160 acres. There are some of us who have a mild horror about country estates when the peace and quiet is disturbed by the murderous screams of rooks and something sinister makes unrecognisable noises in the undergrowth. But it's peaceful inside Glynde Place. The gallery has fine panelling and woodwork made in the late 17th century although the hall, staircase and other rooms were modelled in the middle of the 18th century for Bishop Richard Trevor by John Morris of Lewes. John Morris also built the stable block and the walls surrounding the garden.

Some houses grow old without growing up. Glynde Place, however, has been growing since the 1560's when building began on the flint Courtyard-type plan. At that time the front was symmetrical and subsequently all the windows have been altered with the exception of those in the gables. The house was Georgianised in the 1750s, then Tudorised in the 19th century and must have felt like a woman who has had her face lifted once too often. The Trevor family inherited Glynde Place through marriage with the Morleys in the late 17th century but almost a century later Bishop Trevor remodelled the Great Hall and made a new approach, a monumental one, which is south of the house leading through the stables. He seems to have been a man with grandiose ideas.

All the owners seem to have enjoyed making their mark on Glynde Place and the fact that it has survived more changes than most country houses is a tribute to the skill of the builders. There seems to have been a belief held by all concerned that you can't make a rich cake without a mixture of ingredients. There are a mixture of paintings, too, by Hoppner, Lely and Zoffany. A Ruben's sketch for the ceiling of the Banqueting Hall, Whitehall, is in the house and documents dating back to the 12th century. Even the bronze relief in the Great Hall by Soldani doesn't look out of place. The people who have lived in the house obviously cared about their own contributions, like the birds that still sing in the aviary.

I've met several opera singers, but none more eccentric than the prima donna who only wore her truss when singing Wagner. I've heard Maria Callas hit a wrong note in the middle of *Medea* and beguile the audience, by her acting, into believing that it was deliberate. Valhalla can collapse and nearly kill the lady singing wildly, and probably hysterically, but nevertheless opera dotties unite to compare notes in opera houses all over the world. The most unique opera house in England, for me, is Glyndebourne, east of Lewes in the parish of Glynde. You can get there by driving over the Downs or by boarding a train. You'll have to arrive in evening dress — a must — but this is a small rub to accept when you can enjoy one man's dream of perfection realised on summer evenings. John

Christie created the opera buildings for his wife, who had been a singer.

The atmosphere during the season at Glyndebourne is similar to a fête champêtre within the walled gardens which enclose the buildings and stage tower. John Christie was determined to ensure that the opera house should be worthy of its setting and, acting as his own architect, he collected weathered bricks and tiles to use as building materials which would give the completed project a mellow look. When you walk in the wooded park among the small lakes on a summer's evening, glance back at the high wall of the stage rising above the terrace and notice how the shadows of the tall trees soften the severity of the outline. The perfection which John Christie expected from audiences and performers is matched by the fine stage equipment and the care taken by the local masons and carpenters who built the opera house, excelling in their craftsmanship.

Glyndebourne estate was inherited by John Christie when his father died. There was a considerable amount of money with which to provide a form of foundation where musicians, masons, woodcarvers and ironworkers could exercise their skills as they had done in medieval times. John's father had been capable of building organs, no easy task, and insisted that his son — who had spent 13 years at Eton as a Science master — made use of his education and did something worthwhile with his life. The opera house was the result, evolving through a love of music and as the result of travels to the opera centres of the world.

The high standards of singing, production and stage design have been maintained over the years. New operas are commissioned and performed in addition to performances of well-tried favourites. You can't fail with Mozart, and in one production of *The Magic Flute* the scenery for this delightful pantomime was mobile. Tall pyramids revolved and were moved across the stage by young children, from local families, enclosed within them. The effect was as startling as a teetotaller finding an empty gin bottle under the bed. When one of the pyramids made a wrong stage move and went sharply into reverse it emitted a shriek of surprise that made The Bird Man lose a few feathers.

Verdi, Richard Strauss and Michael Tippett are composers whose operas have been performed at Glyndebourne and who cover a wide span of years and different moods. One of my acquaintances, who loathed anything that required a receptive mind and a keen ear, said: " I've had my ears pierced once, but I never expected to have them pierced again until tonight."

The Palace Pier at Brighton and end-of-pier theatre with the
South Downs in the background

Fishermen's Net Sheds on the shingle beach at Hastings
(Reproduced by courtesy of Edwin Smith)

Piers in winter can be compared
to a rendezvous with old age

Sea-fishing is an occupation which makes your
opponents rise to the bait

The opera was *Ariadne Auf Naxos*, a rich feast for all but the stone tone deaf. Glyndebourne today has an international reputation for fine opera and, as far as the surroundings are concerned, the opera buildings sit like a jewel set in its own enamel. One man achieved his dream and shared it with others. The secret of his success was calling the tune, not changing it.

Men and women with conviction have created great architecture, among other achievements, in our society past and present. The inhabitants of Lewes have been an example to determined conservationists and preservationists. There are only 14,000 inhabitants in the medieval town, set on a hill which is dominated by the remains of the castle. The castle, and the Priory, were built during the barony of William de Warenne and his wife Gundrada after the conquest. King Athelstan had two mints for making money in Lewes before that time and, later in the 13th century, the Greyfriars — the only friars to settle — made the town their centre. The High Street, which cleaves the town like a butchered rabbit, is lined with houses which date back to Georgian and earlier times when Lewes was the country seat for London families. This was the period before Brighton became the fashionable town for an additional family house outside London when the Regent had built his Pavilion by the sea.

Restoration and preservation have retained for Lewes some of the finest architecture in the county. There are churches, but no major ones. Amon Wilds made additions to All Saints, Friars Walk, in 1806 and later additions were made in 1883. The flint church of St. Anne, in the High Street, has a Norman tower, nave and transept as well as a fine South facade, late 12th century. The round tower of St. Michael in the middle of the High Street could also be 12th century, although it is reputed to be a century later. The street facade is late 18th century with windows, in correct Gothic style, made in 1885. The church contains a monument to Sir Nicholas Pelham and his family (1559). The Unitarian Chapel, also in the High Street, was built in the early 18th century and has a knapped flint facade, dour but pleasing, with doorways and an east window of the period. Although the churches can be called minor architecture of their respective periods they contain inside a wealth of Sussex history and treasures. These reveal the unity of family life as well as the unity that existed between local families and the church in centuries past. We must be due for a revival soon.

The castle is one of the landmarks of Lewes. The remains are a permanent reminder of the conflict that once separated

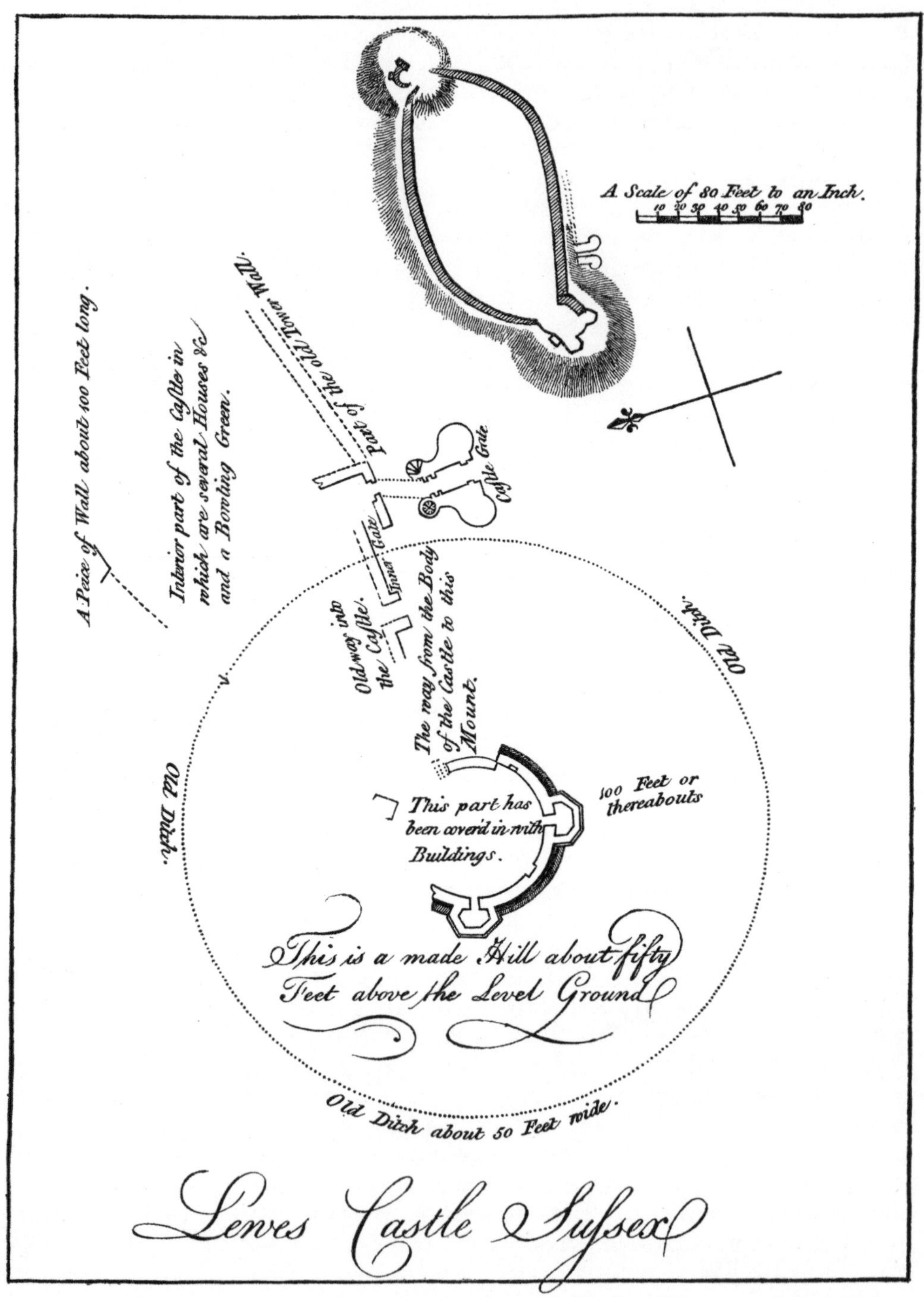

Lewes Castle Sussex

church and barons. In Jacobean times you could help yourself to the stones and the cost for a loadful would have been the equivalent of 2 pence today. No wonder that there is so little left of the castle. There are also the visible remains of the town walls built in the 13th century, two artificial mounds to satisfy the curious, and the tunnel vault which smells like any other haunted place. The approach, through the machicolated archway of the 14th century barbican (one of the largest in England) is intimidating. The pair of round turrets outside, once matched by a pair inside, are constructed of squared flints with cross-slit windows. The groove for the original portcullis is still there today, a reminder that there have been times when the property was not open to visitors.

Lewes, like any county town where there is a generous proportion of 18th century quality building, does have unattractive buildings. We tend to seek out and praise the best Tudor and Jacobean houses, enjoying what they have to offer us whilst turning a blind eye to the architectural stumers that can be justly labelled " fallen buildings ". I find the Town Hall, built in 1893, displeasing and the facade built of bricks that are as red as an unpaid rates demand are unsympathetic to the neighbouring buildings. The Establishment in any field seldom earns its pay despite protestations to the contrary. The County Hall in the High Street has stone panels representing Wisdom, Justice and Mercy chiselled in symbolic defence of any crime of bureaucracy. I've known some splendid officers of Local Government and also a fair number of not so civil servants. Many of the buildings in which they work are monumental rabbit warrens.

I worked, for a short time, in the new County Hall building, a pleasant glass and concrete box that is a dominant feature when you approach Lewes. It overlooks the Downs and was opened in 1969 by the Duchess of Kent at a time when the local inhabitants were calling their new piece of architecture " a white elephant ". My own desk, with its invisible label of Battery Hen Number 77, overlooked the graveyard and every night I passed the Prison, built in 1850, on the Brighton Road. The Prison has round arched windows, low towers flanking the flint and brick facade and some nice old trees. But it is a " closed prison ". Several of my colleagues referred to their surroundings as " the open prison ". You can't be in Local Government for long without realising that you either resign or remain in a state of resignation.

The High Street should be the main delight for connoisseurs of history. The fact that it is not, is due to the continuous stream of heavy traffic that thunders through the narrow winding street, exuding exhaust fumes and shaking the foundations of the fine old houses. The motor car was once our servant but today the roles are reversed and too many people are slaves to the motor cars which they can't afford. People are more important than cars and a definite hazard exists for pedestrians who dare to stumble or step off the kerb on either side of the High Street in Lewes. God help the disabled and aged — the motorists certainly won't! The residents of South Street have devised a simple and effective plan to stop through traffic by blocking the entrance to the street, and providing a new road over land at the back of the street until the new Lewes bypass is built. This decision to form a barricade against traffic noise and air pollution is realistic since by forming a cul-de-sac the residents could, like camels, refuse to break their backs with someone else's last straw.

The word sharawadgi describes a lack of uniformity without loss of order and the word aptly describes the High Street in Lewes. The best buildings include the Shelley Hotel, faced with mathematical tiles and endowed with a splendid 16th century porch. St. Anne's House, opposite the Grammar School, is faced with knapped flints and was built in 1719 although the porch on this building appears to be 19th century. The Freemason Hall, on the north side, built in 1868 is Victorian Gothic and contrasts with Westgate House, decorated with Adam style columns, on the south side. Castle Place was built by Amon Wilds in 1810 and is an excellent example of his early style pilasters, later used on buildings in Brighton. Barbican House is built of Georgian red brick. The variety of elevations in the street is a delight, ranging, in materials, from the black mathematical tiles of Bartholomew House to the rough flint bays and battlements of Castle Lodge. These particular buildings, and many others, sit well together to form a handsome street scene which, I think, is unequalled by any other in Sussex. Where on earth did we lose the knack of combining fine architecture of all styles and periods in the streets of our towns? We have lost it today, I accept, but I sincerely hope that we regain the art before long. Until we do, our streets will remain the reversible overcoats they have become — seamy on both sides.

When you're in Lewes, head for Keere Street, a steep cobbled way that leads off the High Street. It's for pedestrians only, although someone did once drive a horse and carriage down it, recklessly, for a bet. The cottages are pleasant, reminiscent of Polperro, and you can still see the early almshouses that formed St. Michael's Court. When you reach the bottom of the incline you'll find yourself standing outside

Southover Grange, which was built in 1572 for a steward of the Earl of Dudley.

The Lewes house of the Pelham family was a Georgian building three storeys high. Today it is equally well-known as The White Hart, an elegant public house with dining rooms containing Elizabethan panelling and an atmosphere that is as fruity as a Dundee cake. The panelling in The White Hart is probably genuine unlike Anne of Cleeves' House which, architecturally, is Elizabethan at the back and 16th century at the front. If you believe that this building was bestowed on the lady by King Henry the Eighth then you'll believe anything. There is another house in her name at Ditchling and one can only assume that her ghost dealt in real estate. Or, like Anne Boleyn, she may have had a good head for a short while.

The worst feature of Lewes, as you drive out of the town on the road to Newhaven, is the road bridge, a car speckled spanner, and the trail of untidy buildings that recall the littered promenade of a seaside town after an invasion of trippers. This seems to be such a brutal ending to a place that boasts of possessing a Roman road and a feast of fine architecture.

The outskirts of Lewes are a sad echo of George Washington's words: " Few men have sufficient virtue to refuse the highest bidder."

6. Windmills. Harness the Wind

There are rare conversationalists whose flashes of silence make them perfectly delightful. They are as rare as Sussex windmills are today. Windmills that once enlivened the landscape in considerable numbers, grinding corn to be baked into bread.

Decay and fires have destroyed the timbers of which many mills were constructed. Sweeps have slowly rotted and then fallen off the towers like leaves in autumn. Many of the windmills in Sussex were sited on the Downs, where the winds caught and turned the sweeps easily, and they could be seen silhouetted against the cloud-filled sky. Today they are considered to be an anachronism by some people without souls and it is probable that in years to come they will disappear completely like the dodo.

The shapes of windmills are beautiful and, for me, evoke an orgy of nostalgia. Their graceful lines and the variety of detail in their construction has given painters as rich a harvest as the millers who once inhabited them. Windmills were built in times of leisure and their exact ages are as hard to tell as the age of a woman. A great number of Sussex mills are derelict and there are only a few in working order today. When man has tried to conquer nature by harnessing the wind he has invariably lost. The sad sight of the silent sweeps bears witness to this and emphasises the fact that the elements once played a vital part in our lives. Grinding corn had to be a paying proposition and it was, until the wind becalmed the windmill. Nature has had her revenge and left us to suffer that hygienic horror, the sliced wrapped loaf that tastes like nothing on earth.

Many of the finest windmills in Sussex have been preserved, however, by the heritage defenders, a courageous band of people whose concern and care for features which beautify the countryside might benefit future generations. They will, I hope, admire even those windmills which have been converted by their owners to provide living accommodation as a practical alternative to demolition.

You can still see four types of windmill in the county today. Post mills, which have tail poles and talthurs, and those which have only fan-tails. The smock mills which still survive were constructed of timber and were usually octagonal in plan. Tower mills, on the other hand, were built of either brick or stone. The rarest type is a combined wind and watermill and the one at West Ashling is a unique example. You can discover it for yourselves in the flat wooded area of country north-west of Chichester where there are also some attractive timber framed cottages dating back to the 17th century. But the wind and watermill is two mills in one building, each independant of each other like the heads of Cerberus. The windmill works from a trestle on the roof and a water turbine in the building beneath carries out the function of the old water wheel.

Post mills were designed with a wooden casing round the wind shaft and sweeps which revolved round a central post. This type of windmill was topped by a round or pointed roof and there are small square windows, without glazing but with inner shutters to stop draughts, bats and birds, in the main body. The weather boarding and thin metal strips on the outer casing were practical in their design as a means of shedding rain. Sometimes the front and the roof of this type of mill was metalled. There's one at Blackboys, a small one, which was built in 1818. Originally this post mill stood on Glynde Hill until it was moved to its present site in 1868 and subsequent decay has left its mark.

The oldest type of sweeps for windmills were canvas rigged over a framework that allowed the miller to control the canvas when the wind became too strong. Patent self-rigging sweeps were based on a design by Sir William Cubitt in 1809 and were successful because they allowed for adjustment of the sweeps, by weights, without the mill being stopped. They were slower than spring sweeps but were great time-savers in an age that made most of the summertime. Only in retrospect are English summers believed to be hot and endless.

Sussex windmills were designed with four sweeps, about 32 feet in length and with an average span of 64 feet. The sweeps were balanced for safe running. The only six sweep mill in Sussex was at Ashcombe, near Lewes, and that was blown apart in a gale. The fantail on existing post mills turns the sweeps into the wind and they look, to me, like large mechanical doves that have alighted on the top platform. The cap on smock mills, a feature which originated in Holland, is the revolving part that carries sweeps, windshaft and, often, a fantail. The functional design of smock mills — octagonal or hexagonal plan tapering outwards from the windows at the top — reduces the effect of driving rain and this, with the outer covering of weather-boarding, does all that is possible to preserve the fabric of these exposed structures high on their windy hills.

When the sweeps of old windmills snap or decay, it reminds me of the time I broke a porcelain plate, last of the set, and severed a remaining link with gracious living. The most expensive mills to construct, and the most durable, were tower mills. These had tapering brick walls, which were topped with a wooden cap reminiscent of a beehive or one of those woolly caps screwed to shape by a jaunty bobble. The platform on a tower mill is reached through a storm door and at Hurst's Mill, Eastbourne, additional storage space has been provided by enlarging the base of the brickwork. One of the most famous Sussex tower mills, Jack on Clayton Hill, has tarred metal facing over the outer brickwork and was designed with a lower gallery inside to reduce vibration. There are other mills of this type at Stone Cross, Polegate and Patcham although the majority are in West Sussex, where the cement-faced ones were usually painted white.

The windmill at High Salvington, just inland from Worthing, is set on the South Downs 350 feet above sea level. It was built in 1745 and was one of the most interesting since the centre post was made out of a living oak tree which had roots twelve feet deep. At one time, the sweeps were canvas rigged but when the mill ceased to function in 1897 the usual process of decay and deterioration began. The mill was one of the first to be insured against fire by the Sun Life Insurance Company in 1774. If the preservationists had not been determined to keep this robust landmark alive we wouldn't be able to enjoy it today and the views of 70 miles of English coastline that can be seen from it. Actions have always spoken louder than words but these days you have to reinforce your arguments, for saving dying architecture and scenery, by shouting. It's no good complaining, either, you have to stand up and revile those who are responsible for, but indifferent to, our surroundings.

The best post mills, like High Salvington, in Sussex include

Blackboys, Hoad's Windmill, Nutley Mill and Oldland Windmill, Keymer. Nutley is one of the oldest in Sussex and was built at the end of the 17th century in the Ashdown forest amid the heather and the bracken. Oldland Windmill is preserved by the Sussex Archaeological Trust. Hoad's Mill, often called Downs Windmill was built in 1780 and is on the outskirts of Bexhill On Sea. I have a personal preference for Oldland, a small white mill with an octagonal round house, as pretty and delicate a landmark as you could wish to see in the Sussex landscape.

One of my favourite subjects for a painting is Jill, a post mill with a fantail. Jill, with her companion mill Jack, are the famous pair of windmills on Clayton Hill, where they sit like lovers with a field of dreams stretching beyond them. Jack was built in 1876 and is larger than Jill, who was built in 1821 with a dainty, white painted timber frame that was able to withstand the journey from her original site in Dyke Road in 1850. In that year, she was pulled by oxen to the spot where you see her today. She had to wait twenty-six years for a husband whilst flipping her sweeps hopefully. They're inseparable now, weathered but still together, a reminder of Shakespeare's lines: "Men are April when they woo. December when they wed."

The largest active post mill in Sussex is off the Heathfield-Lewes main road and the windmill, Cross-In-Hand, was twice moved from its original site. The first was at Mount Ephraim in Uckfield where it was built by the Lewes Millwrights, Medhursts. The body is entirely metalled except for the tail end which is white weather-boarded.

Chailey smock mill marks the approximate centre of Sussex and it stands on the North Common, where it was restored by Neve Brothers of Heathfield. Other smock mills, like The Old Mill at Battle and Clymping Windmill, have survived because their owners converted them into homes before they became derelict. And on the lonely flats of Selsey you'll find Earnley Windmill. It's a small simple smock mill, built in 1736, covered with tarred weather-boarding and embellished by a unique platform outside, no handrail, and sweeps that are complete.

One smock mill, which is a favourite of mine, is Heinemann's Mill at Rottingdean. It was reputed to have been used by smugglers in the past but today it makes a background for the pitch-and-putt golfers who thwack round it, oblivious of the decaying sweeps and the sorry spectacle of a windmill, well-known as Heinemann's trademark on publications, fading like a ghost from view. Only the seagulls wheel over it, their angry cries borne out to sea. Many mills are reputed to be haunted but these are myths still believed by country people who dispute the fact that owls, who make their homes in old mills, are the instigators of the eerie noises that can be heard late at night. The creaking timbers, too, would account for the tales of phantom footsteps, which, for sceptics, have the same impact as an under-rehearsed thriller in a provincial theatre.

The white weather-boarded smock mill at Rye was rebuilt after the original mill was burnt down in 1930. It makes a complete contrast to the same type of mill at West Blatchington, in Hove, which is octagonal and was built out of other farm buildings. The facing of rough flints and the Catherine Wheel shaped windows date back to 1724 when the mill was built. The mill is supposed to be haunted by a young woman or a broody owl. Smugglers used West Blatchington Windmill to evade the customs officers, presumably on the grounds that a thing of duty is a bore forever.

Ivory towers, like castles in the air, can be expensive to maintain but time has proved that the tower mills in Sussex have been the most durable despite the high initial cost of building them. Jack, on Clayton Hill, mentioned previously, ceased functioning in 1908 and has now been converted into a house. Barnham Windmill is power operated like Mark Cross Windmill on the Tonbridge Wells — Mayfield Road. Halnaker Hill Windmill, on the road from Chichester to Goodwood, was restored by Sir William Bird as a permanent memorial to his wife. A charming tribute that can be seen on the top of the Downs.

Patcham Windmill is the baby of the Sussex tower mills and stands in privately owned gardens bereft of sweeps like a large empty pepperpot. Polegate Windmill, built in 1817, and Stone Cross Windmill, built in 1877, are both near Eastbourne where the bracing air seems to have preserved them as it seems to have preserved the lucky inhabitants of that town. But the remains of Sussex mills stretch across the whole of the county and at least 180 are no longer in existence. One wonders whether any will remain to be enjoyed by those who are developing into good citizens of the Brave New World? Once windmills dominated and enhanced the landscape and a country rhyme reminds us:

> The windmill is a curious thing
> Completely built by art of men,
> To grind the corn for man and beast
> That they alike may have a feast.

Contentment, in the heydey of the windmill, wasn't dependant on great wealth but was satisfied by few wants. Windmills are a reminder of that fact today.

7. Sussex Villages. Stocks & Shares

Most Sussex villages in the past contained houses and cottages belonging to inhabitants whose families had been born there. But village life doesn't seem to have any appeal to young people who want to get on in the world today and, unless our village properties are going to be allowed to fall into a state of disrepair, the subtle takeover by outsiders has to be accepted and welcomed.

There's a slight croak of smoke in the new voices one hears, particularly when they belong to people who have ratted on the race and fled from the cities. You can spot their influence in village streets by the fresh whitewash, the hardwood windows, the carriage lamps, the antique gates and daringly, pieces of modern sculpture where you expect to see hollyhocks. The polished pine and grandfather clocks inside have the unmarked look of furniture newly purchased as opposed to furniture that bears the scars of being handed down from generation to generation. The little old lady with rosy cheeks and a stoop has been replaced by a new liberated woman, who has blue hair and a very pink scalp. The five strings of imitation pearls might be the hallmark of her sophistication and the tell-tale hint of Harrods in all things bright and beautiful.

You no longer have to be brave about sanitary conditions in Sussex villages. The simple life today has supplies of gas, electricity and water and an inside loo of the latest design. The stocks have gone and so has the village busybody, with her small accusing blackcurrant eyes behind pebble lenses. The Barn Dance and the W.V.S. seem indestructible. Even the picturesque sagging roofs, suitably shored, and the restored

Tudor chimneys supporting television aerials reveal that the change in pattern of life in the village has coincided with financial profit. The charm of village worship can still exist for those who have managed to stay in the Houses of the Great, which luckily survive vicious death duties and disappearing domestics. The surviving villagers and new preservationists belong to an age of trust. Developers, and their periphery crowd of agents, belong to the age of cynicism.

The villages, farmsteads and manor houses won't be found along the Sussex coastline but are buried, like treasure, inland from the continuing progress of shoddy architecture that has ruined places like Shoreham, Peacehaven and Seaford. The coast now has the added torture of almost continual traffic which moderates as you progress towards the other side of the Downs. The vernacular style of building in Sussex is composed of brick, tile hanging, knapped flint and timber from the oaks of the Weald. The large forests that existed in the past provided adequate material for timber framed houses, happy reminders of medieval skills. The late Tudor feature of the brick chimney evolved from the central hearth in houses.

Areas of the county have, in the past, been distinguished by their own type of building, a mark of their identity and individuality. The style varied according to the size of a building, from farmworker's cottage to family mansion, but the features and materials in each gave a unity which linked the village together and created an architectural harmony. There is an intrusion of style on the borders with Kent where you may have noticed long low village houses sometimes tarred or faced with kidney shaped flints widely spaced in mortar. Another alien feature to the general run of building elsewhere in the county of Sussex is the facade of squared or knapped flints set closely together. But, in the main areas of Sussex, the recurring architectural materials have been red brick, russet tiled roofs — sporting a fair growth of lichen — and knapped flint facings restrained by red brick quoins. You'll also find the picture-book straw thatched cottages in places like Amberley and, surprisingly, at Bignor. But Insurance Companies are not kind to people who own thatched cottages because of the fire risk and there may come a day when plastic straw is accepted and probably even liked. We already have plenty of plastic weather boarding used on houses throughout the county. It's deceitful, but effective and cheap to maintain.

The Downs enfold small villages protectively. A good example is Fulking, which has charm and character. The Shepherd and Dog Inn sits at the foot of the Downs and not even the car park can detract from the surroundings. Beside the car park, on the bend of the road, is a spring that sheds water from the chalk. Nature has been bountiful and provided the inhabitants of Fulking with a free drinking fountain constantly filled with pure water. And there is a delightful Georgian building, Perching Manor Farm, built of flint and red brick. It's early Georgian, too, with a five bay front. Poynings, just over a mile away from Fulking, has an Early Perpendicular cruciform church, Holy Trinity, built as directed in the will of Michael of Poynings in the 14th century. The church is a dominant feature of this old village and so is the public house, the Royal Oak, a splendid piece of late 19th century architecture with the atmosphere you expect to find in a country inn. By the time you read this it may well have changed.

Pulborough is a strange mixture of suburb and village. The church of St. Mary is a good example of Perpendicular architecture with a tower built in the early 15th century at the same time as the nave and aisles. There's a splendid 15th century cottage among the old houses on the top of the hill, where the sandstone rock provides a natural feature to contrast with the sites of the houses on the low ground.

I have a soft spot for Burpham, which has water meadows — formed by branches of the Arun — spreading between the informal layout of the village. One factor that has preserved Burpham from the fate of other villages, which have suffered the indignities of change, is its situation at the end of a road which stops where the village forms a natural cul-de-sac. You can't go any further once you're in Burpham and it's quite heartening to watch motorists that have strayed folding their road maps with an angry flourish. They don't believe what the maps told them. The village is built on a form of cliff, a bluff, where the small thatched cottages snuggle together so closely that there isn't room for another one to be built. The flint and brick cottages are an echo of the flint cottages and barns in the street at Warningcamp about a mile away. The gardens in Burpham are beautiful, with hawthorn hedges and pink speckled blossom on the apple trees. You can even hear the bees humming with pleasure at the prospect of so much pollen. The church of St. Mary is dignified and plain externally and gives no indication of the vaulted chancel and rich mouldings inside. It was built in the 12th century but there are 19th century additions when the original south transept and aisle were taken down in 1800. This village, high above the River Arun, looks outwards towards Arundel Castle and the town where another, busier world exists.

Lindfield seems to me to be a contrast to Burpham, although

both are Sussex villages. The High Street in Lindfield is a long one and contains some of the best preserved period houses in the county. The village has survived the dangers of accessibility, as opposed to Burpham's point of no return situation, and is near Haywards Heath, which has a very active railway station. At the bottom of the long hill is an attractive pond, a haunt of swans which eye the 18th century buildings regally. Both buildings and birds seem to belong to the same age. Half the houses in the total number that make up the High Street are of medieval origin, stately homes of which Sir Nöel Coward could be justly proud. The group round the church of St. John Baptist, which is mainly 13th century with a 14th century tower and broach spire, is the finest. Church Cottage is a 15th century timber framed building. Old Place is also timber framed and brick nogged, late 16th century with a large south wing added by Charles Eames Kempe, who lived in the house and built the garden pavilion for his pleasure and ours. Thatched Cottage, 15th century, Lindfield Cottage, built of red brick with Shakespeare's bust sitting nobly in the open pediment and Lindfield Place, which is Early Georgian, make an elegant architectural trio. They are outstanding in a village where there are many fine houses built of Georgian red brick or timber framing. Even the cottages, built of Horsham stone and topped by thatch or tiles, are happy reminders of a time when we built with great beauty and practicality. Lindfield possesses some of the finest architecture to be seen in any East Sussex village.

In Tudor times the builders preferred to site their houses facing north and east to take advantage of what they believed were healthy aspects. South winds were believed to encourage diseases and insects although Tudor fleas were probably as irritating as they are today. Woodworm was just as active, too, judging by the state of Tudor timbers. But villagers then, as now, naturally believed what the experts told them and Dr. Richard Russell must have realised this fact when he advocated sea-bathing for health in the 18th century village of Brighton. Even then there were too many vigorous people flirting with imaginary ill health for the greater part of a long lifetime and the same is true today. Living in a village is supposed to encourage longevity and most town-dwellers, like myself, reluctantly accept that butterflies pinned within city walls can only give a last despairing flutter of their polluted wings.

Sussex has many beautiful villages tucked away for the determined to discover. Rottingdean, with its history of smuggling, is today encircled by new housing outside the original village and this continues to grow like a hard skin on a delicate foot. During the lifetime of Edward Burne-Jones and Rudyard Kipling, who lived in Rottingdean, the peace of the village green onto which their houses faced was only disturbed by the angry cry of ducks on the pond and the sound of the sweeps of the windmill turning slowly in the wind.

The roofs of old village houses are often mellowed by orange lichen and the simple buildings are approached by lanes where wild flowers grow profusely. Each village has something to offer visitors, usually a traffic jam these days instead of the honking of geese. It's a different kind of honking, regretably. Alfriston, a picture postcard village, suffers the fate of being too popular in summer when cars and coaches crash the serenity barrier. The wooded valley in which the village sits is invaded by motorists who come to see the rare market cross, the old inns, the flint cottages and the thatched pre-Reformation Clergy House, the first building in the country to be acquired by the National Trust. The cruciform church of St. Andrew, with its 14th century tower, is known as the " Cathedral of the Downs " and, as the parish church, has been the centre of turbulent events including 18th century smuggling and sheep-stealing. In those days the River Cuckmere provided a navigation route from Cuckmere Haven to Alfriston and there were many secret tracks across the hills along which contraband could be taken to suitable hiding places. More sophisticated methods of evading Customs and Excise have been evolved today.

Steyning, the old capital, is really a market town like Petworth and Arundel but it still retains the atmosphere of a village and is dominated by Chanctonbury Ring, which you can see from various viewpoints in the streets and between the houses. Ditchling is still a village, cross-shaped and virtually unspoiled, with St. Margaret's Church as a focal point. The church has been restored but has a 12th century history and a very impressive graveyard where grey December overlooks the Downs. The village has a building called Anne of Cleeves's House, photogenic and picturesque, but certainly in no way connected with the lady whose name it bears. Anne of Cleeves kept her head but those who misnamed the house clearly lost theirs.

Amberley, West Chiltington, Rodmell, Kingston, hamlets like Southease, Piddinghoe and Wilmington are all places of character and each has a unique setting in the Sussex scene. They are serene and peaceful spots and you can laze in their tranquility.

" I wouldn't like to live here, it's too quiet and dull," visitors have been heard to remark in the village pub after a gin or two.

I always wait for them to realise that the local people present are listening and are outraged. Then they add: " But of course it's one of the most charming places I've ever seen."

Their views are usually expressed to the inhabitants at large who regard visitors with the unsettling gaze of well trained gun dogs.

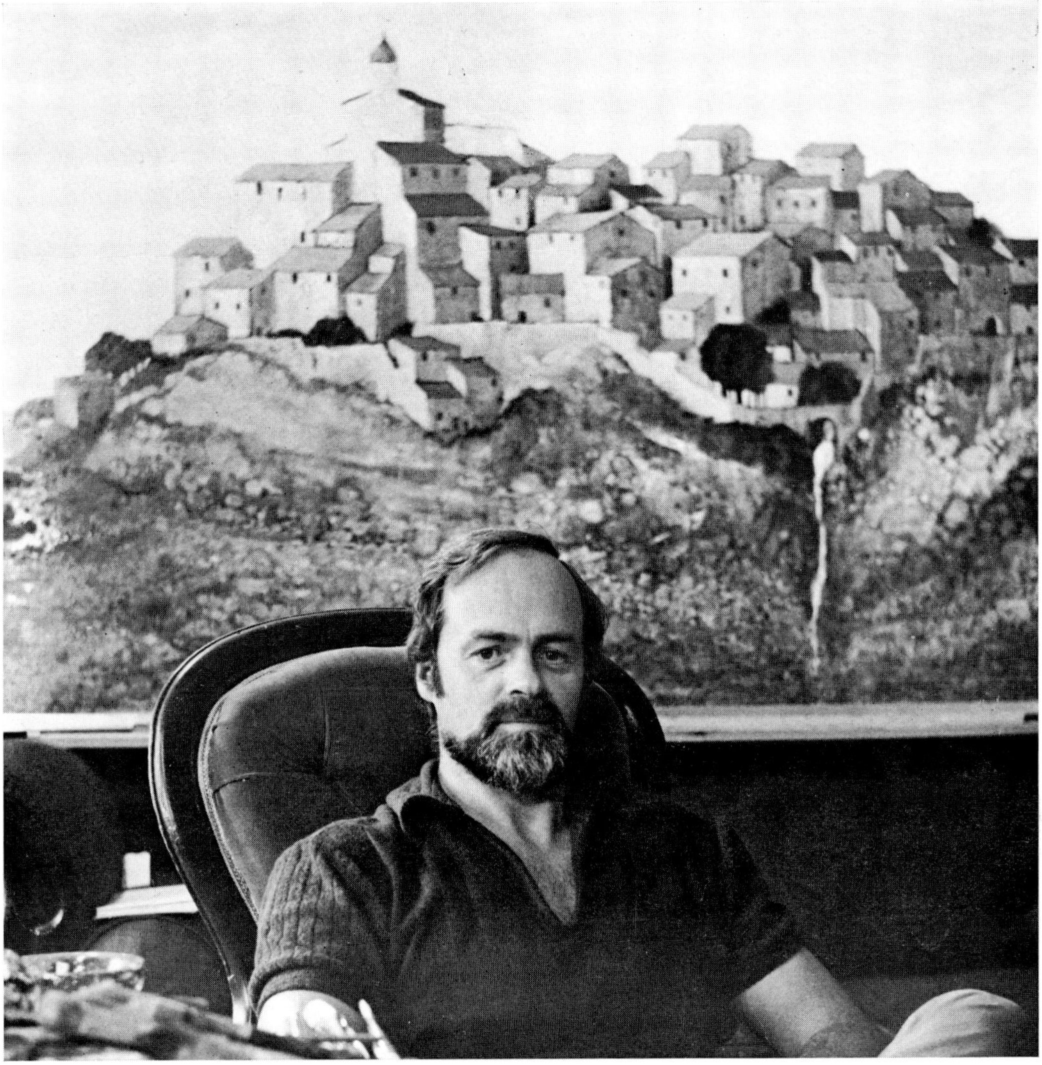

Photograph: Tim Farebrother

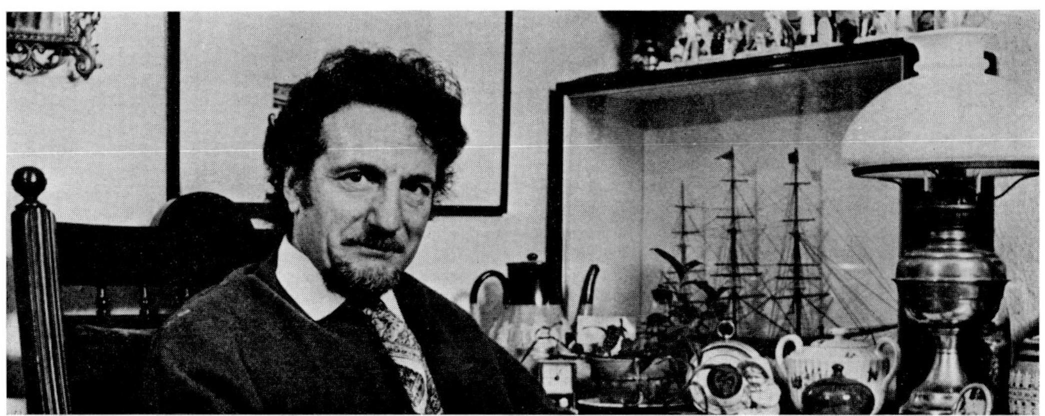

Gerald Parkinson in his studio at Framfield

Norman Battershill in his studio at Shoreham

The Marina at Birdham
(Reproduced by courtesy of Aerofilms Limited)

The Parade Ring at Brighton Racecourse

8. Sussex Gardens.
Last Leaves at Leonardslee

If you think you're too old for growing pains then try cultivating a garden. We, the British, have been called "a nation of gardeners" and most apt that phrase is, too. We certainly love plants and flowers as much as we love animals and home cooking. And home cooking is where many men think their wives should be.

The climate in this country is against outdoor activities all year round but the ardent gardener, a rose red chippy half as old as time, is seldom put off by wind and rain. Ladies who enjoy the creative urge of gardening, equipped with picture hat, Sussex trug and flowered apron may be windswept but have sufficient determination to plant a herbaceous border in a gale when necessary. Some of us don't have much of a garden but take pride in it, while others have acres and pains.

Sussex can be considered as one large garden, a county full of the patterns of nature, the irregularities and man's contributions to the landscape in past centuries from which have grown the villages, hamlets and landmarks. But it is in the gardens created by individuals that one discovers visual surprise and variety; trees of unusual shape or bark, bridges, cascading water, lakes on varying levels as at Sheffield Park and rare shrubs imported during the reign of Queen Victoria.

Earlier, in the 18th century, the pioneers of the "picturesque" were wealthy amateurs with highly developed aesthetic theories. Richard Payne Knight and Sir Uvedale Price were men who had great sensitivity in assessing the subtleties of art and who disparaged the style of chinoisserie in gardens. But it was Humphrey Repton, self styled "landscape gardener" born in 1752, who could present ideas for landscaping and garden layouts on paper with such sureness that his patrons could visualise the final results before work started. His skill titillated the Prince Regent's taste with drawings of Indian projects culled from C. R. Cockerell's fantasies in the English countryside. John Nash, the architect, transformed Henry Holland's classical villa into a marine palace at Brighton for Prinny in 1908 using designs prepared by his partner, Repton. Repton, quite naturally, sulked after his initial rage had passed and was far from satisfied with a payment of little over £700 for his research and ideas. He disliked being cheated as much as he disliked the affectation of symmetry which offended his visual sensibility. His knowledge of architecture and surveying was the basis for that capacity and his views on agriculture prompted the remark: "A rage for farming supersedes the delights of a garden." Repton also considered that parks were lonely places and many people would agree today when solitude and unspoilt landscapes are rare.

Your own garden can offer a place for solitary thoughts and the enjoyment of nature, even the backyard of a terrace house if you wear ear-plugs. Ideally, gardens should act as an extension to the house and provide the maximum use of ground area for family activities. Many of the gardens that are extensions to historic houses in Sussex have been maintained and added to with such care that every prospect pleases. These gardens epitomise the words Pope wrote to Swift in 1736: "Gardening is near akin to Philosophy for Tully says *agricultura proxima sapientiae*." You can discover for yourselves the truth of this statement in gardens owned by the National Trust and on private estates where the skill of experts conserves rare plants, shrubs and trees.

Borde Hill is a good starting point for garden lovers in Sussex and you can study plants and shrubs growing in ideal conditions before experimenting yourself. A trip to Hollycombe is also worthwhile, if you're in search of the unusual, where J. C. Hawkshaw created a woodland garden at the turn of the century and incorporated in it rare shrubs and trees that were the largest of their kind in England. August is a wicked month according to the novelist Edna O'Brien, but that is the time of year to visit Denmans at Fontwell, 5 miles west of Arundel. The walled garden was planned for an all year round display of shrubs and plants to please all tastes. Ultimately there are two kinds of decisions when planning a garden of your own. Those that are expensive to change and those that are not.

Some houses and gardens, like Brightling Park near Robertsbridge, have the added attraction of follies, picturesque additions to the landscape. There are two rotunda in Brightling Park, one of which is 65ft high. The other is domed and has a colonnade. These and the observatory, designed by Sir Robert Smirke with additions by Mad Jack Fuller, have an air of romantic melancholy but were deliberately founded on a good idea. The name and nature of follies defy analysis but they are pleasing adornments to great estates and positive statements of their creators' sentiments. Their effect, on insensitive sightseers, is similar to the effect caused by a flagrant chintze in a Georgian study.

Sherrington Manor at Selmeston, near Polegate, has a garden that has improved and matured over the years, producing fine old roses and large herbaceous borders. The house, mentioned in the Domesday Book, was once moated. The views from the garden are a feast for a painter like the strutting peacocks, Greek symbols of eternity, and the flock of Jacob sheep, dappled by nature. June is the best month to visit the Manor where, surprisingly, dogs are welcome and the car park is free, which is equally surprising today.

May is the best month for visiting Nymans at Handcross when the azaleas and rhododendrons are at their peak and a credit to the gardeners employed by the National Trust. This month, too, is ideal for visiting Charleston Manor at West Dean, the home of Lady Birley. The 15th century Great Barn was used as a studio by Sir Oswald Birley, the painter, when he was alive. Today, restoration has preserved the fabric and it makes a splendid setting for music recitals and poetry reading during the Charleston Manor Festival each summer. On a fine evening you can sit out in the garden at Charleston Manor, where the surrounding trees dwarf people as they stroll across the lawns or wander among the parterres, and find tranquility. You discover another world in what seems like another age and, on a clear night, you can see forever.

Other gardens worth visiting during May include Mountfield Court at Robertsbridge, Souk Lodge near Horsham, Chapelwood Manor at Nutley, Creek House and Pilgrims Cottage at Itchenor (near Chichester). Old Woldringfold near Horsham has a woodland garden that covers more than 4 acres. I find it difficult to select a favourite garden when there are so many fine ones from which to choose. Sheffield Park, near Uckfield, is owned by the National Trust and attracts 81,000 visitors a year. Fortunately the 18th century gardens cover 80 acres so you can find some privacy or jump into one of the five lakes if you dislike crowd formation.

The gardens at Great Dixter, Northam, were designed by Sir Edwin Lutyens, the architect, who included yew hedges, topiary and garden buildings to compliment the 15th century manor house. The gardens are a splendid tour de force and, as at Sheffield Park, there is a rich diversity of planting set in an imaginative layout. Great Dixter and Sheffield Park are successes for the men who landscaped them and for those who maintain them. They have the same splendour that you can see in an ostentatious sunset. But it's corrupting to care about success since neither success nor failure are permanent or important. The best memorial to leave for those who dwell in time, as far as I'm concerned, would be a tree to bless the landscape and shade future generations from the heated moments of their lives. And that is why Leonardslee, and the motive of the man who created it, evokes for me a feeling of eternity.

Sir Edmund Loder, whose family house at Leonardslee was built in 1855, inherited land which overlooked the Weald of Sussex 300 feet above sea level. The wooded valley below the terrace of the house had a stream, which spread out to form a series of " Hammer Ponds " left from the era of the iron-ore industry. These lakes provided water as a motivating power for the hammers and furnaces. Sir Edmund, grandfather of the present owner Sir Giles Loder, also inherited with the estate some of the finest large Californian redwoods and Wellingtonias in England. An ardent gardener, he set out to create a garden which respected the wild character of the surroundings and within which a profusion of colour could be introduced naturally. He didn't employ a professional designer since he believed that he was capable of planning the gardens at Leonardslee himself.

What did he think as he optimistically tackled such a mammoth task? Did he find strength in the belief that a rare and beautiful garden would be enjoyed by the generations to follow him? We can only guess. I think he might have thought: " The best investment on earth is earth." Leonardslee is in the village of Lower Beeding 18 miles from Brighton and the soil is light loam, fairly deep, over sandstone. The valley shelters the land from the north and east winds and lime-free soil is perfect for rhododendrons and azaleas. There is seldom a lack of moisture during our English summers as holiday-makers know to their cost. Sir Edmund might have been amused by the thought that the rainy day for which most of us put money aside usually occurs on holiday.

He started work on his garden in 1887, setting out — as a lover of natural beauty — to produce stunning colour effects. He based his early ideas on banks of massed flowers, particularly rhododendrons and camellias, seen against the existing background of old oak, beech, birch and conifer. There was also bamboo and the curious tree of the Snake Spruce to add a touch of the exotic as well as a " pocket handkerchief " tree with hanging white flower bracts. For thirty years he planted and respected the landscape, adding new varieties of shrubs and experimenting to achieve his aim of giving Sussex a garden that would give pleasure to those who visited it in future years.

Today, no dogs are allowed in the gardens for obvious reasons and no coaches are allowed on Sundays for reasons which are not. The gardens are only open to the public on certain days in the late Spring when the scent in the air and the quality of the blooms can be fully appreciated. After a brief flowering, the colours fade and nature gently changes into a green mantle. It can be compared to a great prima donna who, having sung her final aria, bows to the audience and retires proudly backstage until another season.

The Rock Garden at Leonardslee is an inspired touch by the master gardener. Invalids and the elderly can sit in a walled garden on level ground and enjoy the surroundings. Large rocks and a waterfall provide foil for the plants which are concentrated in this peaceful area. I think that falling water makes a beautiful sound. Add to this the hum of bees and the scents of nature and you have the secret of Leonardslee, where Jeanie Anscombe found inspiration for these lines:

> In the promise of a primrose
> late and lovely moments lay,
> beyond the summerlanes of Sussex,
> in the simple fields of yesterday.

Portraiture, which is eloquent, was born from the noble Renaissance dream of man. True eloquence in a garden consists of planting all that is necessary and nothing more.

9. Beside the Seaside. Piers of the Realm

The seaside resort offers pleasure which is urban and social. The architecture and ephemera owe their conception to the enthusiasm of the medical and literary advocates of the late seventeenth century in Britain when the sea was considered to be unhealthy and a resting place for sailors. Even the aristocracy knew that you couldn't get blue blood from a stone at the seaside.

Dr. Whittie, of Scarborough, published his views on the benefits of internal and external use of salt water in 1660, and claimed that it cured gout. A century later, dipping in the sea was cited as a cure for practically every illness, including mental sickness. Dr. Richard Russell published his book on the benefits of sea-water in 1750 and moved from Lewes to Brighton in 1753 to promote the seaside. The Royal Albion Hotel today occupies the site of his original house. Benjamin Beale, a Margate Quaker, invented a bathing machine, a timber hut on wheels with a door at each end, in the same year that Dr. Russell came to Brighton.

The search for health was the making of the seaside industry and when George III emerged from a bathing machine for a dip in the English Channel at Weymouth in 1789 the seal was set. Horses and riders gambolled across the sands and some bathers undressed inside the new huts as they were drawn by horses to the edge of the sea. The decorous were covered with a canvas " umbrella " before being dipped in the sea. The dippers were bathing attendants who held the bathers' head and hands before forcibly submerging them in the water. Husky women, like Martha Gunn, were tyrants whose unwelcome embrace overcame any resistance but some men, in hired boats called cobbles, preferred to plunge into the sea naked and leave the ladies to struggle in their huts. Onlookers, with telescopes, soon realised that there was less to most men than met the eye.

The coastal villages of Sussex affected by the new fashion for bathing were quick to seize on the commercial opportunities offered from 1760 onwards. Brighton, Worthing and Hastings

found bathing and fishing equally profitable and where fishing
cottages met with bathing machines prices were inflated for
visitors requiring service and seafood. Eventually the wealth
being accumulated by other towns prompted Eastbourne to
adopt bathing machines despite an initial reluctance to do so.
Royalty usually leads fashion by the nose, and when the Prince
Regent set his marine palace in Brighton, Londoners adopted
the town as their main resort.

The Chain Pier at Brighton was opened in 1823, a fanciful
piece of engineering by Captain Samuel Browne, later
knighted, that extended the land into the sea for 1,134 feet. It
was a liberating idea, a cast iron suspension bridge on
ornamental stone columns supported by piles. The Brighton
Pier Company had received the blessing of Parliament when
an Act was passed on 1822. The capital investment of £27,000
enabled the Company to provide a landing stage for coastal
steamers, and a sight for those who liked to promenade out to
sea. The costumes of the Norman visitors, with their high

conical hats and brightly coloured clothes must have been a strange contrast to the sober clothes of the locals watching the initiation of the first passport business. Custom-house officers examined each passport of male arrivals, but the women were taken to an outhouse and searched by pipe-puffing females, authorised Government officials, the fore-runners of Social Insecurity. Messengers were also sent by local hotels to solicit custom, which added to the annoyance of the tired and irritable visitors who had paid £1.75p for a cabin and £1.05p for steerage on the twice weekly service. There must have been stormy moments but none so stormy as the night in December 1896 when the Chain Pier, through neglect, was destroyed by the fierce sea. The Palace Pier was built to the west of it in 1899.

Salt water was never kind to cast iron although 19th century piers were achievements for the engineers who pioneered the material. No two piers were alike and they encouraged the holiday mood in those Sussex towns fortunate enough to own a pier. Brighton had two piers at a time when they were not considered extravagances by a cost-conscious society. The West Pier in Brighton was built in 1866, four years after Worthing had built its pier. Eastbourne followed in 1870 at a time when the expanding middle classes and prosperous tradespeople visited resorts made accessible to them by the railways. Resorts rivalled each other in the elaborate detail and entertainments which their piers could offer the public, although it was the railways who encouraged the public more than beaches or piers. Hastings built a pier in 1872. At that time most of the piers on the Sussex coast had domed pavilions, amusement arcades, weighing machines, automata, souvenir and sweet kiosks, bars, baths, reading rooms and sheltered seats. There weren't many piers along the Sussex coast but the few that existed were choice.

The railways, as well as coaches, enabled "hoys" and artisans to infiltrate the new resorts on the Sussex coast and elsewhere. The old fishing villages, where the windows of cottages faced away from the sea, expanded with Marine Terraces, Parades, Drives and Esplanades along which shrubs were planted. Even cliff walks were treated to a new type of landscaping to provide sheltered spots in which to rest. Bandstands ornamented the front, like those at Eastbourne and Hove, with a lacey froth of ironwork at odds with the military precision of the performers. Assembly Rooms, theatres and circulating libraries met a demand that expansion produced. Fortune hunters and matchmakers abounded, as well as retired military and naval men for whom the sea air and changing population provided a new lease of life. The season, May to

October, attracted the pickings of wealthy society, who didn't have to build a reputation on what they were going to do. Their reputations followed them, like the gulls following fishermen.

When you were beside the seaside in the 19th century the entertainment consisted of French string bands, nigger minstrels, tumblers and Punch and Judy shows. You could buy fruit, cakes, balloons and hatguards on the beach. The barouches and landaus were drawn by prancing horses along the seafront roads, where rich women could parade their clothes and lovers. The solitaire diamond might be tennis-ball size and provoke the remark: "Isn't that really dignified?" It wasn't, but a healthy vulgarity was expected at the seaside, which appealed to both the rich and the poor. They had mutual tastes in the love of gaming, high living, women, horseplay and colour. The Sussex coast can satisfy all of those loves as far as I'm concerned, and when people talk of a generation gap today they need reminding that the only thing that kept our elders pure, in the past, was fear. Money and sex are still great motivating forces and neither has ever suggested purity.

True to the Victorian character, the selection and success of a resort depended on visitors finding a moral tone to suit their tastes in surroundings and people. If you didn't care about people or the holiday spirit, then you found a place in Sussex to practice the current fever for botany. You ran the risk of being stung severely by nettles or jellyfish for being an isolationist. Seaside resorts were labelled according to the social category which they encouraged. Londoners seeking gentility and quietness went to Eastbourne, Bexhill and Bognor Regis. Those who went to Hastings, Seaford and Worthing preferred small scale resorts devoid of vulgarity although at Worthing you were liable to find seaweed 2 to 3 feet high on the beaches where it was whipped up in tons from the sea bed. Rye, which is the nearest equivalent to St. Ives to be found in Sussex, today attracts potters. In the last century, its Bohemian atmosphere and the salty speech of sailors attracted artists. Brighton, as always, was noted for its hedonistic delights and also appealed to Jewish visitors, who stayed to increase the existing population of 80,000 in the 1860's.

Today, the planners and developers have decided that modernising the existing facilities of a seaside town is the only way to ensure survival. Piers, which some people consider to be anachronisms, have received cool glances from local authorities who leave their future in the hands of the property Companies and businessmen who own them. Attendances on piers have dropped dramatically in this century and, as enter-

tainments, some are no longer a viable business proposition.
The Companies are not philanthropic societies and do not
expect to subsidise piers which cater for an unprofitable
minority past-time. The rape of piers seem inevitable but you
can't expect those to whom they appeal to lie back and enjoy
it. The West Pier at Brighton needs £800,000 spent to restore
the ailing structure and those who shout loudest about this
sorry state of affairs, or sigh nostalgically over port and lemon,
are not likely to raise that sort of money easily. Nostalgia,
unfortunately, is a small town on the outskirts of wishful
thinking.

The arteries of our coastal towns have been hardened by
traffic that will continue to increase. Buildings in the centres
of seaside towns have been left to decay, or demolished to
provide space for car parking or entertainment centres, those
monuments to " the good life " which has always seemed an
ad-man's dream. To many people, including myself, it recalls
the words of William Blake: " You never know when you've
had enough until you've had more than enough." Meanwhile,
the insensitive tower blocks continue to rise from the depths of
unimaginative minds, which are as unfathomable as the sea,
and fail to express the spirit of seaside architecture. Architecture, for Sussex-by-the-sea, was a splendid 19th century
legacy of buildings that fulfilled the basic requirements of
strength, gaiety and sharp outlines. Stucco, expensive to
maintain, gleamed in the sunlight and still looked splendid in
bad weather. Decorative cast ironwork, flamboyant in design
and tough in use, was an apt choice for the seaside as you can
see today on houses in the Regency terraces and squares at
Hove and Brighton.

Current building materials used for projects in St. Leonards
and Hastings would make Decimus Burton and his father turn
over in their graves. New buildings at Eastbourne, where they
face the sea, have a rare quality of unrelieved ugliness. Bognor
Regis, in its architecture, seems to have acquired the frumpish
air of Frinton and today's builders seem content to erect
sombre constructions for benefit-conscious society and forget
that liveliness is needed in seaside towns. Far too many
Sussex resorts have failed to preserve the spirit of the seaside
in their trimmings and have offered, instead, Municipal
Perpendicular. You can't feel high spirited when our coastal
towns are more concerned with sewage outfalls and oil
polution than they are with amenities.

But take heart! On one pier, a notice warns visitors: DON'T
THROW PEOPLE BELOW. It's heartening to be reminded
that the air on piers is still so bracing.

10. Sussex Characters.
Landscape with Figures

Folklore is created from the traditional beliefs of people who live happily in the remoteness of country districts protected from development and sophistication. Some of these people haven't had a formal education and most of them outlive their dogs. They judge life by their experiences and are unspoilt by artificiality. Their impact on the county can be found in proverbs and folk songs, the expression of cheerful people whose idea of a perfect life is their own. " Tomorrow is a post-dated cheque," they tell you, " but today is cash."

The population of Sussex today, based on the 1971 census, is 1,241,332 an increase of 163,815 in ten years. East Sussex, including the three county boroughs of Brighton, Eastbourne and Hastings, has 750,312 people and West Sussex 491,020. Since 1951 the population has increased by nearly a third from 937,339 inhabitants. A large number of the $1\frac{1}{4}$ millions are never going to be famous and those who do succeed in accomplishing a mention in county history will probably do so before they reach their level of incompetence. The memorable characters, like those in the past, will be fortunate in having natural and instinctive gifts that can achieve remarkable results.

Nancy Mitford has said : " Life goes on for so long that if you do anything you become quite good at it." You certainly do if you have an awareness of human folly and vanity, coupled with a knowledge of what is really going on in the world about you. Characters that are remembered with pleasure are not usually puritanical and very rarely respectable in the ordinary sense. Perhaps this is why painters are generally good company? Sussex seems to provide a good background for painters and writers to record their impressions and stimulate personal emotions. Their achievements can be the result of natural talents, cultivated and developed to satisfy themselves first and others later. A painter is interested in his next painting and the public is interested in the one that has just been completed.

I have always enjoyed the apocrypha of famous last words. They're a final record, like Robert Bridges' instruction: " If Miss Constance Masefield calls, tell her I am not at home." Most characters, and the creators of characters, have made observations on life that reflect their own personality. You'll remember Mame, that unique aunt in Patrick Dennis' family, who observed: " Life is a banquet but too many people are starving." Sussex families, notables and characters were recorded in a large book, published in 1865, compiled by Mark Anthony Lower. The choice of people mentioned in that

mammoth piece of work, *The Worthies of Sussex* sub-titled *Biographical Sketches of the Most Eminent Natives or Inhabitants of the County,* was a personal one, quite indiscriminate, resulting in a happy mixture of the unforgettable and forgettable. There is a parallel on occasions when one is invited to an elegant black-tie affair and has to stand for hours smiling politely or enquiring about unknown guests. You will be rewarded by vivid and surprisingly cruel personal histories.

Sussex history was made by people who probably didn't realise they were making it as well as by men and women of outstanding talents. History is made every minute of the day so there's a chance for all of us. The morning headlines are stale news by evening but the whims, peculiarities and doings of people loosely labelled " personalities " seem to become sagas and are avidly read in newspapers where the quoted word becomes gospel. But as reading matter it's relaxing and acts as an antidote to the fevers of wars and violence. All characters are distinctive marks imprinted in time.

Phoebe Hessel was a woman of character and courage who had a strong desire to live expressed in a readiness to die, if necessary, for love. We associate her with Brighton, where she is buried in St. Nicholas' churchyard, but she was born in Stepney in 1713. When she was fifteen, a strapping girl with a deep voice, she fell in love with a soldier named Samuel Golding who was under orders for service in the West Indies. Phoebe enlisted in another regiment bound for the same place. They must have had short-sighted medical officers in those days because she served with the regiment for 5 years without being recognised as a girl. She fought in the Battle of Fontenay in 1743 and was bayonetted in the arm. She was also at the Siege of Gibraltar at the same time as General Elliot, later Lord Heathfield, who adopted the name of a Sussex village.

Miss Hessel was discharged from the army when she admitted that she was a woman and received a Chelsea pension. Love can never be learnt but it can be sustained as Phoebe Hessel knew when she finally married her first love after he had been wounded in service. Twenty years and nine children later, Samuel died, leaving his widow free to marry a fisherman who lived in Brighthelmstone which was then a fishing village. When Phoebe's second husband died she still sold fish from her donkey and cart until it became a financial liability. In 1806 she was discharged from the work house and became a street seller on the corner of Old Steine where you would have seen her in all weathers wearing a brown serge dress. Her basket was loaded with apples, bullseyes, gingerbread — they were men, naturally — and toys. She became Brighton's oldest inhabitant in 1814 when she was 99. She celebrated the Coronation of George the Fourth in 1821 by riding in a carriage with the vicar of Brighton. This was the year before her death, at the age of 108. A remarkable old lady, who was born in the reign of Queen Anne and who, when she died, didn't believe in the prevailing fashion of abusing George the Fourth.

Thackeray, however, was quick to speak in defence of the fashion: " One of the best physicians our city has ever known is cheerful, merry Doctor Brighton. But what myriads of Londoners ought to thank him for inventing Brighton!" He spoke of a different attitude to Sussex coastal towns where today there has been far from idle talk of turning them into counterparts of Las Vegas and the Californian seaside resorts. Progress is invariably accepted as a factor of survival even when this entails exchanging one form of hell for another. Sir Nöel Coward, who found Sussex " terribly piece full ", has already given his own views on Las Vegas: " One of the most respectable towns I've ever known. The people are so preoccupied with gambling that they've no time for minor vices." Gamblers may be colourful characters but they take all the fun out of kibbling kippers.

Fame and notoriety have often shared the same bed of circumstance, a situation familiar to writers. Sussex has been lucky in attracting the attention of writers with staying power. Those who did stay left their own distinctive marks and have enriched our literature. Some were born in Sussex like John Fletcher, a dramatist in the reign of Queen Elizabeth the First. Rye, where Fletcher was born in 1576, has aspects of Shakespeare's England in streets like Mermaid Street where the houses, built on rising ground, have their rooflines silhouetted and light is angled against the leaded panes. The streets are a strong contrast to Rye's surrounding scenery of marshland which Henry James, who lived in Lamb House at the top of Mermaid Street, enjoyed in his later years. He may have found solace gazing across the lonely landscape that can be seen for so many miles on all sides of the port that became a town. Seclusion is valued when you're famous and Ellen Terry found a place, a cottage by the side of the Strand Gate in Winchelsea, once a sister port with Rye. Actors and writers seem particularly prone to a lack of privacy in their private lives although most accept the fact gracefully, preferring to be looked over rather than overlooked.

Hilaire Belloc was fortunate in being the type of man who could hold his public at arm's length. He wrote that the South Downs " were the centre of all good things and home of happy men." Belloc was an advocate of Roman Order and the charm of the county he wrote about had not then been subjected to the harsh reality of what planners consider are modern needs. His love of Sussex would have been wounded by the sight of villages and towns where advertising, those eye-patches of commerce, and insensitive wirescapes and street trimmings have wrecked harmony. The worst architectural misdemeanours make me sigh nostalgically for the village life that Walter Wilkinson recorded in his book *A Sussex Peep Show*. " There it lay beneath us as simple as ever, with the smithy and heaps of old iron still in the centre of the village, with children in pinafores playing in the village street, and men in their shirt-sleeves tidying up the sweet-smelling flowers in the riotous gardens."

Horace Walpole invented the word serendipity, the faculty of making happy discoveries by accident while searching for something else. He had no love for Sussex, however, dismissing it as Saxon and an area of England that dampened curiosity. Even Herstmonceux Castle, a rather grand building that one would have imagined had appeal for Walpole, aroused tart comment: "The chapel is mean and small; the Virgin, and seven, long lean saints, ill done, remain in the windows; there have been four more which seem to have been removed for light." If Horace Walpole actually said: "I do not seek, I find ", then he didn't find anything to please him in Sussex.

Shelley, the poet, was born in Sussex at Field Place near Horsham. His home was a mansion that epitomised gracious living. Perhaps the happy atmosphere of Shelley's birthplace, with its gardens and mature trees, was conducive to a poetic nature? When Sir John Squire wrote: "But Shelley had a hyper-thyroid face " he suggested the reason for the poet's complexity of character. Happiness and tranquility of mind eluded him while others, more humble and less gifted, found them in the surroundings he had forsaken. Shelley was like a lone green elm bearing one golden bough, a mind tinged by autumn.

People of genius are sometimes more akin to amateurs than to professionals but Charles Dickens, who liked to give readings from his works to audiences of up to 1,000 admirers in the Town Hall, Brighton was a professional man. He was perfectly content to be in the centre of a crowd, exercising his theatrical talent and using his fine voice to great effect. His ability to convey emotions was an asset which appealed to the Victorians who were never slow to show their feelings almost as dramatically as the characters he brought to life for them. Dickens wrote *Dombey and Son* as well as the greater part of *Bleak House* when he stayed at hotels — The Old Ship, The Junction House and The Bedford — in Brighton. Even now I can visualise him writing steadily in hotel rooms with the bed unmade behind him. The atmosphere would have had the same impersonal quality of theatrical digs but held the simplicity and warmth Dickens expressed vividly in the Micawbers' way of life.

Horace Smith and his daughters, Harrison Ainsworth, Thomas Hood, Samuel Rogers, the Reverend Sidney Smith, Henry Buckle and Charles Kean were all part of the early Victorian literary scene in Brighton. Anna Sewell, born in 1820, was authoress of the sixth best-seller in the English language. The book, *Black Beauty,* revealed an incredible understanding of horses and their care and could only have resulted from acute observation aided by the advice of stablemen. Anna lived in Brighton for ten years but moved to Lancing in 1845. The lameness that overtook her at the time was restricting but she drove her father, in a pony and trap each day, to Shoreham Station from which he commuted. Isaac

Sewell, her father, seems to have been able to cope with a wide variety of jobs and after a further move to Haywards Heath the family moved on again to Chichester when Mr. Sewell was appointed manager of The London and County Bank. But it was not until 1861, when Anna eventually left Sussex and was dying at her final home in Norwich that she dictated to her mother those parts of her book that she was unable to write herself. The book that brought her fame, *Black Beauty,* germinated from the seeds sown in Sussex and the manuscript was sold to a Norwich publisher for £20 in 1877, a year before her death.

Illness also affected the life of another writer associated with Sussex in the 20th century. Virginia Woolf was hypersensitive about her work and at Monk's House, Rodmell — near Lewes — she wrote her later novels. These included *The Voyage Out,* a work that caused her to have a breakdown which led to her suicide, from drowning in the Ouse, in 1941. She worked, on average for fifteen hours a day. Her writing was volcanic, demanding from her great passion and concentration. The tensions which her writing caused and the intensity she gave to it were at odds with the peaceful surroundings of the water meadows and Downs where she walked for an hour or so each day. Mrs. Woolf's superior intellectual views justified the word " highbrow " and Edward Albee's play, written in the 1960's, was appropriately titled: *Who's Afraid of Virginia Woolf?* But Virginia Woolf was a writer whose ideas were in advance of the times in which she lived. Her book, *To The Lighthouse,* was first published in 1927. When the book was reprinted in 1965 with critical acclaim 22,000 copies were sold and justified the faith of her husband, Leonard Woolf, who was also a writer.

Life in Sussex was not particularly happy for Eric Blair, better known as the writer George Orwell. He wrote an essay *Such, Such Were The Joys* about the five years from 1911 which he spent at St. Cyprian's, a preparatory school at Eastbourne. The school was burned down, although not by Orwell, and he became successful when *Animal Farm* and *Nineteen Eighty-four* were published. Both books have aspects which reflect the loneliness and misery that he claimed to have experienced in Eastbourne. Orwell, who was sensitive and suffered from an inferiority complex, eventually won a scholarship to Eton as did a contemporary of his, Cyril Connolly, the author and critic. St. Cyprian's, despite the attacks made by Orwell on a school which he considered encouraged snobbery and uselessness, would seem to have groomed two literary giants whose characters owe something to their years in Sussex. Many

The Portico, Goodwood House
(Reproduced by courtesy of the Trustees of Goodwood House)

Sheffield Park, where the gardens were laid out by Repton before 1794
(Reproduced by courtesy of The National Trust)

Batemans, Rudyard Kipling's house at Burwash
Built by an ironmaster in 1634 and derelict when Kipling found it in 1900
(Reproduced by courtesy of The National Trust)

Charleston Manor at West Dean painted by Sir Oswald Birley in 1935
The Festival, held at the Manor each year, encompasses all the arts
(Reproduced by courtesy of Lady Birley)

people who suffer from an inferiority complex are inferior, but George Orwell proved that he was not.

Some writers reveal the unfamiliar aspect of their subject to give it a new dimension. There are also writers who see the characters they create through a veil of irony than can expand to assume a significant quality, like caricature. Graham Greene achieved both these qualities in *Brighton Rock* which, when it was published in 1938, roused anger in Brighton against the violence and potential crime that the seaside resort seemed to encourage. Graham Greene was unperturbed outwardly, since he had skillfully observed and recorded in fictional form the atmosphere of free-spending and thuggery that existed in the 1930s when this was associated with Brighton race-course and the dance halls of the period. I met Graham Greene in the 1960's when he was staying with his brother in Brighton and believe that he, like the late Evelyn Waugh, made social comment on free society where it is safe to be unpopular. In the 21st century the refusal to compromise may be recognised as a national virtue.

Risk is the incubator of art and can strengthen character. Baxter, the Lewes printer who pioneered the field of colour printing would have known this since he, like most innovators, was years ahead of his time. *"Baxter's Select Sketches of Brighton, Lewes and Their Environs: forming a series of Engravings on Wood with Descriptions* was published by J. Baxter, Proprietor, 37 High Street, Lewes in 1827. The outstanding craftsmanship of Baxter enabled him to spread art among the masses despite the difficulty of executing fine prints at that time without the aids we have today. He manufactured his own printing ink when existing inks didn't suit his purpose and by using the roller in printing processes he reproduced famous works at prices that those of modest incomes could afford to buy. Baxter also recorded contemporary scenes that no longer exist and he, like Cobbett in his *Rural Rides* (1822), managed to convey the essence of the county in print and words.

Art Nouveau, for those who dislike it, is a style that makes a fuss out of nothing. At the end of the 19th century, the appearance of *The Yellow Book,* with illustrations by Aubrey Beardsley, would have aroused the same anger from prudes that some publications arouse today. There will always be people standing on the Gaderene slope as a futile barrier against the onrushing swine and there will be others who can only be happy in a swinish way. Malcolm Muggeridge has pointed out, shrewdly, that what is really funny cannot be objectionable. Aubrey Beardsley was witty at a time when humour was often tinged with malice. He was born at 12 Buckingham Road, Brighton and between the ages of 20 and 25 was acknowledged as a superlative artist in the medium of black and white drawing. His sensual illustrations covered a range that included the works of Aristophanes and Juvenal, Malory's *Morte D'Arthur*, Wilde's *Salome* and the poems of Sir William Watson, who lived in Rottingdean. Beardsley produced drawings that were sometimes religious. At other times he seemed intent on producing drawings which bordered on the indecent. All of them were incisive and elegant, creating an illusion of space that can be compared to the clear-cut line of the Downs set against sky and fields. The general feeling created by Beardsley's work was that it portrayed distortions of nature, often human nature, and like an exotic bloom his life ended suddenly when he was only 25 years old.

Life provides the ingredients of happiness, but the mixing of them depends on us. The Victorian era provided a pageant of Sussex characters from the shepherds, richly described by Bob Copper in *A Song For Every Season,* to musical hall artists, actors, advocates and painters. The Victorians, when they were not rushing about the county on botanical surveys, yielded an extraordinarily high number of Sunday painters, enthusiastic amateurs who filled sketchbooks with landscapes, seascapes and whimsical fantasies based on popular art. Their inspiration, in many cases, could have been Constable. John Constable was not particularly fond of Sussex but he brought his family from the smoke of London to Brighton nearly every summer from 1824 to 1830. He found the clear light of the seashore satisfactory and his vision encompassed more than the immediate scene in front of him. The light and colour in his works of the period were far in advance of the rigid styles of that time. He was a poet with paint. Go and see for yourselves the painting which Constable achieved from watching the people strolling along the Brighton seafront, under a stormy sky, with the houses and Chain Pier in the background. The work hangs at the Tate Gallery in London. The sense of excitement it conveys is stimulating and although John Constable may not have cared for the general air of Brighton the setting served him well.

If you were a member of the Earp family your interest in painting would have been as certain as death and taxes, both of which concerned the Victorians. The Earp family were exceptionally gifted when it came to using a paint brush and their impressions of the coastal scene, boats, piers, sunsets and storms have left a pleasing record of the age in which they lived. Their works fully justify the expression " paintings for pleasure " and although their impressions can be seen in Sussex art galleries, particularly Brighton Art Gallery, you can still discover watercolours by H. Earp and F. Earp in local antique shops. The family output must have been prolific. A descendent, St. John Earp, continues the family tradition of painting today but with a distinctive style that places his work high on the list of outstanding modern painters.

Sir Frank Brangwyn produced many large scale paintings and was at the height of his fame in 1930. He lived in Ditchling where he was commissioned to paint 18 panels for the House of Lords as a memorial to members who had lost their lives in World War One. When five of the panels were completed and submitted to the Royal Fine Arts Commission he was stunned by their views that his paintings were unsuitable. Sir Frank, for whom financial recompense was no comfort, had believed that the panels would provide the culminating point in his career. No painter feels secure and the rejection of his work can leave a deep wound. Even Eric Gill, who also lived in Ditchling, was subjected to the indignity of modifying the sculptured figures he had produced of Prospero and Ariel over the entrance to Broadcasting House in London. Eric Gill was also responsible for the Gill Sans lettering we use today and was equally talented as a typographer as well as a sculptor.

The 'thirties provided painters, architects, fashion designers and craftsmen with a chance to express themseves freely because there was an absense of any well-defined trend or movement. Rex Whistler, who designed for the theatre in this period, was a delightful character who died tragically in Normandy in the Second World War. Many people remember his designs for the play *Pride and Prejudice* in 1936 but he is permanently remembered in Sussex. He painted murals in the Officers' Mess of the Welsh Guards when they were stationed in Preston Park Avenue before D-Day. His work has been described as elegant and witty, and indeed it was, as you can see from the allegorical mural painting that hangs today in an upper room of the Royal Pavilion, Brighton. The mural, " HRH The Prince Regent Awakening the Spirit of Brighton ", depicts a lecherous looking gentleman awakening a voluptuous nude. He has the pale, dampish look of somebody who could have spent their lifetime on the seashore and a leer that suggests that there was nothing more fun than a man.

Jean Anouilh, the playwright, has pointed out that the object of art is to give life shape. Both art and literature have recorded past and present worthies in Sussex. The character of our towns, particularly those with noble Regency buildings, and our villages where the needs of ordinary people have given

them shape, remain an historic link between generations.
Architects like Amon Wilds and his son, Decimus Burton and
his father, Sir Charles Barry and, today, Lord Holford have
succeeded in giving expression to their own personalities and
beliefs while benefitting those for whom they built.   The
changing landscape provides material for our painters, Norman
Battershill, David Humphreys, Lesley-Ann Gorton, Valerie
Mackenzie, Francis Russell Flint, Gerald Parkinson, Sylvia
Parkinson, Dion Pears, Margaret Milnes, Dorris Kirlew,
Dorothy Coke, Robert Earley, Matt Bruce, Stephen Stevens,
Monica Leighton Hicks, Charles Evison, Margaret Norton,
Jeanne Courtauld, Pauline Brown, Norman Black, Keith Jordan
and D'Oyly John.   A feast of names and all painters who have
painted their impressions of the county in this century.   Jill
Pryke, noted for her fine pottery, uses the colours of nature and
continues the tradition of craftsmanship.   Galleries like the
Arun Art Centre at Arundel, The Ditchling Gallery at Ditchling
and others in The Lanes at Brighton are ideal places for painters
to show their work and make contact with the public.

Any selection of characters is a matter of personal choice.
The difference between people who have achieved results by
using natural and instinctive gifts and those who have not is
summed up by the words: " I did not have time."

11. Sporting Life. Insiders and Outsiders

Plebians and patricians had several tastes in common; a love of gaming, high living, women, horse racing and colour. Today, there is an inner darkness, that comes in a commercial age, which tends to tarnish the silver cups of sporting life.

Sporting events in Sussex occur during all seasons, ranging from folk customs of stoolball and pancake races to International Show Jumping at Bolney. Horse Racing, County Cricket, League Football, Sea Angling, Regattas, Cycling Championships, Amateur Athletics, Lawn Tennis, National Speed Trials and Golf Tournaments cater for a variety of interests on land or on the coast. There are casinos and saunasiums, even a Dolphinarium, for people in pursuit of pleasure. " The national sport of England is obstacle racing," Sir Herbert Beerbohm Tree said, when questioned on the subject. " People fill their rooms with useless and cumbersome furniture, and spend the rest of their lives trying to dodge it."

The essence of Sussex can be enjoyed on the village green, and Gold Cup day at Cowdray Park has something of the village green in its atmosphere. The rich are different, as Scott Fitzgerald knew, and you have to be rich to play polo. Ponies cost from £600 upwards and you need at least three of them for a match. Polo originated in Persia but was also played in parts of India, on open ground or in village streets. Any number of players could take part. The sport of " hockey on horseback " was brought to England in the 19th century by British Cavalry officers when they returned from India. There are now only 17 clubs in Britain and at Cowdray Park, on the Easter Monday meeting, insiders know each other by the set of their stetsons or by the handstitched gloves worn by the ladies. If you hate polo, you won't want to count points in the uncomfortable seats, which encourage counting sheep to shorten the waking hours of a dull meeting. It's hard to sleep, however, when the Midhurst Town Band starts playing as an alternative to the records, which are usually slipped discs. The annual meeting is an event, although polo matches are played each week from April to August. The setting is magnificent, with beeches, chestnuts and oaks as a background for the impressive ruins of Cowdray House, built in 1530 and burnt down in 1793. There are excellent stables in the area, and well-trained dogs that don't let you down.

Horse racing is like a love affair, which involves only one person but needs six legs. The breeding of weight-carrying horses was at its peak in Sussex during the reign of Henry VIII, a heavy man who could exhaust ten horses during a day's hunting. Armoured soldiers, equally heavy, needed horses for mobility and laws were passed to ensure that breeders concentrated on providing their King with a stock of weight-carrying horses to the detriment of lighter breeds. The heavy horse was used through the centuries, and its steady pace was ideal for drawing carriages, waggons, and carts. Man and horse both have an instinctive dislike of being overtaken when racing. The sport began in Arabia, where racing the Southern stock of early Arabian horses was one of the pleasurable pastimes of eastern rulers. The Romans brought organised racing to Sussex during the years of their occupation. The hippodrome was an arena, for flat racing, where tests of skill and stamina took place.

There are a number of courses to visit in Sussex today where the standards of racing are high. Fontwell Park, 4 miles west of Arundel, has Flat and Steeplechase meetings from February to November. Ringmer, 3 miles north-east of Lewes, has point to point during early Spring and at Plumpton Racecourse, near the downland village, you can watch steeplechasing from February to May then September to December. Plumpton Place, the 16th century manor house with a moat, was restored by Sir Edwin Lutyens, the architect, during the 1920s. Brighton Racecourse, which stretches along the top of White Hawk Down and overlooks the sea, has flat racing from May to September, for 16 days. There are still hawks hovering overhead for unwary sparrows as there were when racing started at Brighton in 1783, the year when the Prince Regent visited the town for the first time. In 1805, the year when the Royal Stables on the Pavilion estate were under construction, the race was won by the horse Orville, an outsider which the Prince had bought a year earlier from Christopher Wilson.

Christopher Wilson was nicknamed " Father of the Turf " in recognition of his work in abolishing the more unsavoury aspects of racing. The silver-gilt trophy, a classical vase designed by John Emes and made by the Prince's silversmiths, had been won by Orville but was given to Wilson as a princely gesture. The cup is now on show in the Royal Pavilion at

Brighton. Racing in Brighton had a bad phase in 1849, the year when the Queen's Cup was withdrawn. The aristocracy and royalty stopped entering horses when the crowds, who attended the races on the first three days of August following the Bank Holiday, became insufferable. The railways encouraged criminals and unruly types to try their luck on the racecourse where pickpockets, confidence tricksters and thugs had a field day. A new stand, costing £6,000, was built in 1851 as a sop to the important racegoers, but the damage had been done and it was not until the 1880s that Brighton races regained their popularity.

The Duke of Richmond, who gave up racing at Brighton in the middle of the 19th century, was fortunate in possessing " Glorious Goodwood ", the course which was the finest in Sussex. The course remains the finest in the county today, and the meeting on the last Tuesday in July is one of the main events of the year for racegoers. The first recorded meeting, however, was in 1801 and eleven years later the Gold Cup replaced the Silver Cup Race. The Gold Cup is the oldest surviving race at the meetings held at the course each year, and was originally held in April. The Goodwood Stakes, dating back to 1823, and the Stewards Cup Race, which dates from 1834 when the race was a 6 furlong handicap, can be watched from the comfort of the grandstand today. A century ago, the races had to be viewed from vantage points on the roofs of carriages or on horseback. Goodwood, at one stage, survived on one meeting a year like Ascot, but four days racing are not an economical proposition when buildings and the course require expensive maintenance. There are races now on eleven days, during July, August and September, to maintain the standards expected by the third Duke of Richmond and Mary, his Duchess, when they started racing at Goodwood at the end of the 18th century. The racecourse originated when the Duke, as Colonel of the Sussex Militia, and his officers were not allowed to ride against each other in the neighbouring Petworth Park after a difference of opinion. An alternative place for competitive racing had to be found. " It is difference of opinion that makes horse races," Mark Twain wrote. He had described, exactly, the circumstances that made Goodwood famous.

Those people who are not addicted to cricket consider it to be an organised way of spending time idly. I've never understood why criticism should be levelled at such a pleasurable way of spending time in the fresh air, particularly when you frequently hear those breathless words: " We saved five minutes." Those minutes saved will eventually be lost again in sleep, like the time taken for a cricket match. County Cricket week in

Hastings occurs during July and there is also County Cricket at Hove during that month of flies and white flannels. Sussex has been one of the cradles of cricket. John Marshall, in his book *Sussex Cricket,* has provided an excellent history of the development of cricket in Sussex with the story of Sussex County teams before and after the institution of the County Championship.

In 1637, Henry Brand of Selsey was whacked on the head by a cricket bat wielded by Thomas Hatter and later died murmuring: "Who won?" The 17th century was not noted for its gentility in sports and you could take your choice of tortures from hunting, hawking, ninepins and cricket. All were lethal pastimes, and none was suitable for the squeamish or the delicate. The Earl of Sussex enjoyed cricket matches, one of which was played at Dicker in 1677. The sport had spread through the county by the 18th century and, although cricket did not originate in Sussex, there were many sportsmen in south-east England who enjoyed bending the willow on village greens. The famous team of eleven men at Hambledon, in 1750, were probably the innovators of "county cricket", which progressed to the Championship and Test matches. Richard Newland, a Chichester surgeon, captained a team at Slindon in those early days of the sport and his nephew, Richard Nyren. was a member of the Hambledon team.

The village green, for cricket, the church and the pub have always been focal points of community life in Sussex, as they have been in other counties. The Sussex County Cricket Club was formed in 1839, although attempts had been made to form a regular club three years earlier. The beginnings of the club were not particularly spectacular but members must have realised that new ideas, like wars and love affairs, are easy to begin and hard to sustain. The early matches were probably comical by today's standards, particularly when they were played by smokers versus non-smokers, batchelors versus married men and family teams. Parochial fun, certainly, and respectable sport for an Englishman. Sussex teams have played cricket on four grounds in Brighton and Hove since the 18th century. The Prince's Ground, later Ireland's Gardens, were the first grounds used in 1791 but they were closed in 1847. The area is known as Park Crescent today. The Montpelier Ground, now Montpelier Crescent, had a variety of names including Lee's Trap Ground, Temple Fields and Lillywhite's Ground. It was opened in 1834 and closed ten years later. Brunswick Ground, Hove's " cricket ground by the sea " was between Third and Fourth Avenues and opened in 1848. This ground, too, was closed in 1871. Today, the fourth county ground at Eaton Road in Hove, opened in May 1872 and at the end of the 'sixties the Club proposed replanning part of the land to provide a new pavilion and better facilities for members.

Teams of Sussex cricketers have played on grounds at Horsham, St. Leonards, Hastings (at The Central Cricket Grounds), Lewes, Eastbourne (at The Saffrons), Chichester and Worthing from 1853 to the present time. It's a long record of hard hitting. Tom Box, wicket-keeper and inn keeper, was a professional in spirit and ran the Brunswick Cricket Ground in conjunction with the Brunswick Hotel in Hove until 1863. Box was a splendid looking man, who was described as being " erect and commanding " until he collapsed from a heart attack and died after changing the scoreboard. He was one of the characters of local cricket, like many of the Sussex bowlers of which three, James Lillywhite, James Southerton and Richard Fillery, left their marks also. Sussex batsmen did not predominate in the 19th century, and you can visualise the tall, bearded players knocking the bails off the stumps with greater ease than they could score a boundary. I suspect that their eyes, in those days of gaslight, may have found difficulty in focusing on a moving object like a ball.

1895 was the year that started what has been called the Golden Age of Sussex Cricket. The batting improved when men like C. B. Fry and Ranjitsinhji, called Ranji for short in his long association with Fry, came on the scene. The two men made runs as fast as a splinter can in tights today. Their association would have been interesting to watch, the elegant silk-shirted Indian Prince, who became the ruler of Nawanger, and the solid Oxford trained captain, meticulous in his conventional dress but swift to move when necessary. Fry created a record for a run of centuries in 1901 and total runs of 3,000. The combination of oriental skill and English solidarity was formidable and, at the beginning of the 20th century, they created legends for cricket fans to recall during the misty winter months when they walked briskly along Hove Seafront.

No cricket was played during the First World War but a great deal was played at Hove during the Second World War. Service teams met county teams. Service cricketers included sailors on leave from HMS King Alfred and members of the Australian Air Force, who were billeted in Brighton and Hove hotels. Cricket, not surprisingly, was a boost for wartime morale and was a sport which couldn't be disrupted by the tragic events in Europe and the Far East. A sport in which players had to have unity, in turn united the crowds who were able to watch. I don't think that we shall see more spirited cricket than was played in those war years even though the standard may be higher today.

Two men have given Sussex cricket a boost since the 'fifties. One was David Sheppard, a Cambridge blue born at Reigate, who captained Sussex in 1953 and raised them to second place in the table, a feat which recalled their success at the turn of the century and in the 'thirties. Sheppard was the greatest Sussex captain in recent years and, when he took Holy Orders, the loss to Sussex was a gain for the church. The other benefactor was the Duke of Norfolk, Patron and Past President of the Sussex County Cricket Club, who allowed a benefit match to be played for George Cox at the private cricket ground of Arundel Castle. The match, in 1949, was the first of a series that have become annual events, during which you can almost hear the Union Jack fluttering in the wind, particularly when the Duke of Edinburgh's team meets the Duke of Norfolk's team for a joust.

Familiarity can breed content, and contentment, for some of us, is associated with fine summer evenings in familiar surroundings. I was staying in Midhurst when I played stool-ball for the first and the last time. The game is as basic in purpose as a cut-throat razor and almost as dangerous. Stoolball in Sussex was popular until the 18th century when cricket supplanted it. Both games have 11 players each side, but stoolball requires an underarm — some say underhand — technique for bowling and the bat looks like a fugitive piece of gear from table-tennis. You have to have strong nerves when you bat, because the wicket is a 12inch square stool raised on a stake over 4 feet high. It is dangerously near eye-level. The rules, which I found deceptively simple, allow you to be ousted by the term " body before wicket " assuming that you have the courage to cover the target. " Leg before wicket " involves only minor injuries in cricket, but in stoolball, played by those rugged villagers round Midhurst, you don't have a leg to stand on if you go out on the field with an innocent mind determined to stake your chances on the stool. Dishonour is infinitely preferable to a month spent in the county hospital.

There is no connection between stoolball and football, for which it's the size of the ball that counts and not the surprise of it. Brighton and Hove Albion Football Club, the " Albion ", play in the Second Division of the Football League at the Goldstone Ground, Hove, where supporters expect a home win. The club was founded as Brighton and Hove Rangers in 1900, and the present name was adopted a year later. The team entered the Football League in 1920 and, after a tough start, finished fifth in the League in the 1923-24 season. Supporters of the club express their opinions of form or players forcibly, in print and in the unprintable, but one has to assume that a proportion of all football fanatics are against everything all of the time. The Albion applied for re-election to the League in 1948 and made the Second Division, for the first time, ten years later. When the team dropped to the Third then the Fourth Division, pubs in the area of the home ground were kept busy helping supporters drown their sorrow during the 'sixties. But by 1966 the Albion were back in the Third Division again and they had 35,000 spectators for their game with Chelsea in the F. A. Cup selection at home. By 1970, Pat Saward was appointed as manager and, although the performances of the team in recent years have been controversial, the Club has provided Sussex with a football team that doesn't collapse like a tent onto the field. Brighton and Hove Albion fought a magnificent battle back into the Second Division, after a 10 year absence, in May 1972.

County Open-Air Sports, either on land, sea — or under the sea — are increasing in popularity every day. One of the reasons for this is the advances which have been made in equipment to make the pursuits easier. Another reason is the improvement in techniques of modern sports and the interest stimulated by television and radio in sports reports. BBC Radio Brighton, the local radio station in Sussex, went on the air in February 1968 and has provided commentaries of sporting events for people who are confined to their homes. The service covered an area from Peacehaven to east of Worthing when it began, but has now reached as far north as Lewes. But the original limits are being extended. Most tastes in sport can be satisfied in Sussex. Tennis Open Championships are held at Devonshire Park, Eastbourne, during June and the Open Lawn Tennis Association Tournament, which includes the West Sussex Championships, is played at Bognor Regis Lawn Tennis Club during August.

There are open competitions for tennis, bowls, golf, and sailing at Seaford throughout the summer months. Golf courses, some with a 19th hole, are good at Seaford, Brighton, Lewes, Newhaven, Hawkhurst and Lamberhurst. Cowdray Park has a Club Course. Cooden Beach Golf Club was the starting point for a campaign which has been mounted to designate all golf courses in Sussex as nature reserves. The Sussex Naturalists' Trust have pointed out that many golf courses are virtually nature reserves through which a golfer may drive a ball straight down the middle without damage to wild ducks. Golfers are usually respecters of nature until they find themselves in a bunker.

Anglers in Sussex can fish in the sea from boats, beaches and piers. I'm full to the gills with fishing stories, particularly when I've had to eat another angler's words. An appetite for sea fishing can be satiated, however, at Worthing, Shoreham, Newhaven, Seaford and Brighton. Anglers who prefer the peace and solitude of river fishing can find a peaceful perch on the banks of the Adur. The alternatives, for river fishing in Sussex are stretches of the Rother, the Teise and Powdersmill Pond, near Battle. Great Sanders Reservoir, at Sedlescombe, is a pleasant place to fish. Oliver Goldsmith told Dr. Johnson in 1773: "If you were to make little fishes talk, they would talk like whales." There are certainly plenty of little fishes in the freshwater fishing areas of Sussex but no whales. The River Ouse, which is tidal from Newhaven to 4 miles north of Lewes, is an excellent source of freshwater fish and there are other equally good harvesting grounds among the streams and reservoirs in the area of the River Cuckmere. The International Sea Angling Festival is an annual event at Hastings in November and, if you have a nose for fish, then that is the occasion to cast your hooks and bread on the waters.

There are indoor sports, as well as outdoor sports, in Sussex for evening athletes. Bingo combines social contacts with a mild form of gambling. It also brings out, in frail old ladies whose handbags exude a faint aroma of camphor, hidden pension money and the battling strength of Henry Cooper. One-armed bandits have hypnotic charm for some of us. The machines, which originated on Coney Island, USA, in the 'twenties, are more ruthless than the taxmen for relieving people of their money. Casinos opened in Sussex when an Act of Parliament was passed, in 1960, making gambling legal. The Act was amended in 1963. The location of casinos in the county is restricted, and selected centres on the coast are at Brighton, Portsmouth and Ramsgate. When the chips are down, the profits are up for those fortunate towns. In the early 'seventies, casinos were required to provide an entrance at street level and The Metropole Club, at Brighton, which opened on the first floor of the Hotel Metropole in 1962, was replanned to meet that regulation. The character of the casino now lacks the opulent luxury that was created in Monaco's casino by Charles Garnier, for the Prince, in 1856. The Metropole Club and The Sergeant Yorke Club, for Brighton's gamblers, are in the modern manner. The functional approach has the disadvantage of creating a mood of bagatelle and chips instead of caviar and breaking the Bank. Sir Hiram Maxim, inventor of the machine gun, gave indoor sportsmen sound advice in 1902: "The most sensible advice that can be given to would-be gamblers is — don't!"

In order to gain the benefit of any sporting life, from cycling with the Crawley Wheelers to walking alone on the wild side of Sussex, you need time on your hands and the energy to help pass it. You may, like me, have an interest in the majority of sports. On the other hand, you may have no true interest in sports' events and prefer to be a bon viveur, in which case the Pancake Race at Bodiam on Shrove Tuesday might appeal to you. Pancakes date back to a time before the Reformation, when eggs and butter in households had to be used up before Lent. The last day for fun and games before Easter was Shrove Tuesday, when the haste to make use of perishable foods resulted in batches of pancakes being made. The race at Bodiam is only open to women, whose ability to run and toss their target makes any winner worthy of selection as Sportswoman of the Year. Too many people in sporting life look back regretfully, or look forward hopefully while the present is offering them flowers.

12. Castles and Country Houses.
Private Lives in Public Property

You don't have to be one of the ruins that Cromwell knocked about a bit to appreciate the castles of Sussex. Lewes, the Norman castle with a shell keep; Pevensey, a gaunt landmark like Yorick's jaw enclosed by Roman walls and Herstmonceux, a partly moated and restored 15th century building better known today as the home of the Royal Greenwich Observatory. Hastings castle and Battle Abbey are linked by their history, stone gemini opposed in principle and related by fact.

Arundel Castle, home of His Grace The Duke of Norfolk, is an ancient castle rebuilt in the 18th century and altered in 1890. The portraits and furniture, however, date from the 15th century. The castle is a magnificent one but the leading National Trust attraction for visitors, about 94,000 a year, is Bodiam. This spectacular moated castle was built by Sir Edward Dalyngrigge " for defence of the adjacent country and resistance to our enemies." The entrance is on the northern side and this much photographed facade is one of the finest examples of mediaeval military architecture in the county.

One of the largest moats in England surrounds Michelham Priory, owned by the Sussex Archaeological Society. This Augustinian Priory at Upper Dicker, near Eastbourne, is one of the top historical attractions in Sussex and is visited by about 66,000 people a year. The Priory was founded in 1229 and has an Elizabethan wing. There is also a late 14th century gatehouse to make a splendid combination of architecture of all periods in one setting. Architecture is part of our daily lives whether we realise it or not.

Castles, like castles in the air, are expensive places to maintain. We're fortunate in having some of the finest country houses in England sited in Sussex and they're a major contribution to the visual arts. The majority of these houses are open to the public for part of the year. Visiting other peoples' homes has given me great pleasure, particularly because they reveal a great deal about the character and tastes of their owners. You may feel that some of the historic places you visit are not furnished as true homes should be. One must be patient, however, with people whose ideas differ from one's own. They're entitled to their ridiculous opinions.

PETWORTH HOUSE. 5½ miles east of Midhurst at the junction of the A 272 and A 283. Owned by the National Trust.

Age only matters when one's ageing, although one can still feel 18 when you reach 80. Petworth is a fine old town, very old, with cobbled streets and a giant chestnut tree that creeks in the wind like my own rheumatics. The town is best seen from the South Downs and foothills because inside the streets there are a series of 90 degree bends, like Midhurst, and a very un-English quality. There are good buildings of all periods mixing harmoniously, lions lying next to lambs, and suggesting that this well-preserved virginity may signify a limited capacity for love. Like the spindly spire on the church by Sir Charles Barry.

But it's the house that draws visitors rather than the church and Market Place. This rich, patrician building, devoid of unnecessary ornament is a jewel set in its own enamel — the surrounding parks and the interior enrichment. Some people read books to kill time, others take walks. A walk in Petworth Park, landscaped in the late 1750's by Capability Brown, is an experience in timelessness. The views have the same values now as they had when they were first considered in relation to the landscaping. The magic is so powerful that you'll find yourself reluctant to leave the grounds.

Petworth House is a massive building, 300 feet in length. It was originally a castle — enlarged from an existing manor — which belonged to the Percys of Northumberland after a licence to crenelate was granted in the early 14th century. They used it as a resting place after the exhaustion of the northern marches and the court intrigues. I see the male members of the household as truculent camels refusing to break their backs with someone else's last straw. Elizabeth Percy, an orphan and last of her line, had a series of miserable marriages. Her motto seems to have been: " Marry in haste and repeat at leisure." Elizabeth found peace and happiness at Petworth and when she married Charles, the 6th Duke of Somerset (whom many people disliked) in 1682 the old house and its dependant buildings were remodelled.

The magnificent west front was Charles' creation — no known architect has been named although the work has French elements — and he refitted the existing 13th century chapel.

The Duke of Somerset was a proud tyrant and he must have worn an Unhearing Aid since none of his servants dared speak to him. He was a militant high-brow whose energy, when setting about the decoration of the main rooms, should have made the Recording Angel take up shorthand. He gave Grinling Gibbons, in 1692, a free hand to create the masterpiece of the Great Room (now known as the Grinling Gibbons Room) in which the lavish decoration and all forms of art mingle with birds, beasts, fruits, flowers and musical instruments. The detail is exquisite; the wealth of carving unique of its kind. Carved eagles and scrolls surround the portrait of Henry the Eighth — an early copy of Holbein — but each portrait is set in lavishly carved panels made up of cupids, wreaths of roses and festoons of ivy surmounting doves.

The Duke of Somerset and his wife were not blessed with good looks as we can judge by their portraits under the cornice. Elizabeth was probably the sort of girl who, while being made love to, would be thinking that tomorrow was the day for rearranging the flowers. Personally, I see them as two people who found happiness in a marriage of companionship and, from this, wished to give to others a permanent reminder that beauty is in the eye of the beholder. Beauty and the lust for learning can't be allied, but the Somersets were responsible for the Marble Hall, the Vandyke Room, the Beauty Room (ironically) and the grand staircase in the south-east. A wealth of paintings hangs on the walls. Elizabeth used her money with panache, making Petworth a vehicle for her taste and skill. Do study, for instance, the carpet — woven at Exeter in 1758 — which covers the Marble Hall. When she died, however, the inheritance she left passed back to the Northumberland line and came to the Earl of Egremont.

George Wyndham, 3rd Earl of Egremont, was a delightful eccentric who defied convention. He disliked the formalities and snobberies of 18th century country house society and believed that taste and leisure should be free of convention. He was, by nature, a born batchelor despite marriage, being blessed by ample finances, a philanthropic nature and shrewdness. He was more dined against than dining but believed in the motto: "Live and let live." Lord Egremont's charm was his "putup-ability" (as Sir William Beechey described it) and as a patron of the arts he increased the existing collection of old masters at Petworth. His major achievement, however, was the creation of a gallery where the work of contemporary painters could be displayed as well as statuary. He was one of the earliest collectors of paintings by Turner, who was encouraged to use Petworth and to paint in an atmosphere free of worry. Turner

Chichester Festival Theatre
Architects, Powell and Moya
(Reproduced by courtesy of The Architectural Review)

The Congress Theatre, Eastbourne, completed in 1963
Architects, Bryan and Norman Westwood and Partners

The Royal Pavilion at Brighton
The architect John Nash added icing sugar to the cake already created by
Henry Holland, whose original building is inside.
(Reproduced by courtesy of The Royal Pavilion Art Gallery, Museums and Public Libraries)

The Shell House at Goodwood
decorated by the second Duchess and her daughters in the 1740s
(Reproduced by courtesy of Chichester Photographic Service Ltd.)

painted views of the house and grounds, fine work which reflected the happiness and inspiration that patronage provided. He made sketches of visitors, full of humour, and a witty sketch he called " Teasing the Donkey ", a favourite of mine.

In the golden years at Petworth, from 1800 to 1837, Lord Egremont was immune from the tiny patter of criticism, realising — I suspect — that any fool can criticize and many of them do. His vast wealth provided us with masterpieces by Turner, Romney's portrait of the Egremont family and work by English painters that include Lely, Gainsborough, Reynolds and Hoppner. There are Vandykes, a Holbein, a Franz Hals, a Rembrandt and a Claude Lorraine. His high spirits could have been due to a youthful outlook, drink and good health, which, despite marriage, he never put behind him.

Petworth House in Lord Egremont's time was a place where his friends could come and go as they pleased, an hotel which embraced the riches of the country without charging. How different to Switzerland, where they've built a wonderful country around their hotels. Petworth stands today as a living memorial to the men and women who created it, learning, earning and yearning. That is, and was, the basis for the good life.

BATEMANS, BURWASH.   13 miles south of Tunbridge Wells, off the A 265. Owned by the National Trust.

Too many actions carry a price-tag today but when Kipling wrote: " I've taken my fun where I've found it, an' now I must pay for my fun " the words had a bitter sweet quality. The King Lear of literature understood the feelings of simple people.

Rudyard Kipling once lived on our doorstep at The Elms, a high-walled house facing the Green in Rottingdean. There was no privacy for him, however, since he was a celebrity and therefore prey to sightseers. Serendipity struck when he discovered Batemans. " What the *Bandar-log* think now," he wrote in The Jungle Book, " the jungle with think later." He growled threateningly at interlopers before deciding to stalk away into the private jungle that awaited him at Burwash.

Batemans, the yellow sandstone house at Burwash, was Kipling's home for 32 years. When he found the house in 1900 it was derelict. He restored it with affection and filled the rooms with his possessions, many of which were gifts from all over the world. He found peace and wrote *Puck of Pook's Hill* and *Rewards and Fairies*. The house now contains the Kipling Collection, although the author's study is the usual dusty memorial that dead writers have preserved in their memory. But the spirit of the man is in his works.

Kipling loved Sussex and how well he recorded it in sentences as well as poetry. "Our blunt, bow-headed, whale-backed Downs" describes their strength. Landmarks, too, were not forgotten: "And the Long Man of Wilmington looks naked towards the shires." Burwash is a village in the heart of Sussex, where winding lanes lead you through the place the locals have nicknamed "Kipling' Village". The house is in the valley with wooded hills on one side and the village on the other. The dark yew hedges glisten with the dew of morning and iron gates, resembling spun lace, are a reminder that an ironmaster built the house in 1634. The gabled roof is crowned by a stack of chimneys and the main facade, almost symmetrical, is as golden as the dreams that only sleep could have given Kipling.

The right wing that once formed part of the house has gone. But the mullioned and transomed windows remain and so does the porch, which is round-arched and decorated. The River Dudwell flows on nearby, whispering to the reeds and the house that have known each other for over 300 years at a time when Shakespeare had only been dead a short while. Life, for some of us, doesn't pass too quickly, but flows on peacefully with high and low water from time to time.

Bonar Law came to the house during the First World War to tell Kipling that his only son, 18 years old and a Lieutenant of the Irish Guards, would not return from France. Kipling said to him: "You have come to tell me my son is dead." This was after the Battle of Loos and must have been a bitter moment for the poet of the British Army, whose patriotism and love of the Empire had made him world famous. The name of John Kipling, his son, can be seen on the stone lantern of the peace memorial by the church. In the porch there are the wooden crosses brought from the battlefields of France and on a medallion the Latin words that sum up the futility of all wars: "Who died too soon." Even Kipling's chauvinism wavered in *Gentlemen Rankers* when he wrote: "God help us, for we knew the worst too young."

Kipling will be remembered for his gentler moods and the poetry that records the county in which he lived:

> Each to his choice, and I rejoice
> The lot has fallen to me
> In a fair ground, in a fair ground,
> Yea, Sussex by the Sea.

There is also one great poem in *Recessional,* which contains a salutory warning against imperialism. He found poetry in people and nature. He found romance in ruggedness, a word that you scarcely hear used today. There's a Rudyard Lake in Staffordshire where Kipling's parents became engaged and it seems probable that this was the origin of the name they christened their son. Lockwood Kipling, his father, was in the Indian Civil Service and when Rudyard was 17 he went out to Lahore after being educated at the United Services College at Westward Ho! He had published, when he was 21, verses in the *Civil and Military Gazette.* These were satirical and were called Departmental Ditties. After travelling to America, when he was 23, he returned to England.

Barrack Room Ballads, when published, came up to his admirers' expectations. So did *Kim, The Jungle Books* and the *Just-so Stories.* There were criticisms of his poetry during his lifetime and after his death. He was accused of being politically minded while at Batemans and his verse was called undignified. But he was convinced, and I think rightly so, that lines in poetry must always fit the message they carry. He also found, while living at Batemans, an alternative type of writing to works which in his early years had been an expression of Victorian barrack-room life.

Kipling, like his fine old house, was individual and original. The house today is furnished as it was when he lived there. No country home is complete without a dumpy little figure sighing in the large kitchen wishing she was back in a small, warm, overcrowded room baking bread. That's how I like to think of Mrs. Kipling. But go and see for yourselves the visible expression of a man who was excited by the world-wide influence of the British race. Kipling was a man who found hope in the faint notes of a banjo when no other music could be heard.

The last words are his: " He laughed one of those thick, big-ended British laughs and don't lead anywhere."

SHEFFIELD PLACE AND SHEFFIELD PARK. 4 miles north west of Uckfield on the A 275. The gardens are owned by the National Trust.

Autumn is the most beautiful time of the year when you don't have any leaves to rake. But when you do, like the gardeners in Sheffield Park — situated midway between East Grinstead and Lewes — you have an outsize problem coping with the rare trees and shrubs. Even the fine waterlilies that grace the five lakes have to be tended. In nature there are no rewards or punishments; there are consequences, according to H. A. Vachell.

But, to me, Sheffield Park is a romantic's paradise. Did you know that earlier in the century the park was famous in cricket history because the Australians used to open their season there? The Bluebell Railway, home of vintage engines and coaches, also runs between the park and Horsted Keynes for five miles and attracts railway enthusiasts from all over the world.

The house in Sheffield Park — once known as Sheffield Place — is Gothic Revival in style and was designed by James Wyatt, the Controller of Public Works and Buildings in the reign of George the Third. His patron was John Baker Holroyd, first Earl of Sheffield, whose friendship with Gibbon the historian was based on the belief that the most precious things in speech are pauses. Gibbon wrote *The Decline and Fall of The Roman Empire* in 1776 when he was 39, without any pause, and with great effect on the literary world of his time.

Sheffield Place is an 18th century mansion, extremely large with three main fronts. The building sits on an ashlar base and has buttress-shafts and pinnacles on the entrance side and pointed arches under gables on the garden front. The effect is clumsy but eerie. You may have seen these qualities used to good purpose in Jack Clayton's film of " The Innocents ", an essay in haunting atmosphere that benefits from the architectural qualities of the house and the magnificently landscaped gardens which were laid out by Repton before 1794. The ground-work, however, was carried out by Capability Brown in 1775 and there have been modification in the 1930's. The gardens cover 80 acres and the 5 lakes are on different levels which, like life, form an unbroken succession of false situations. Even in early summer, when the air is perfumed by azaleas, honeysuckle and rhododendrons, one has the uncanny impression that something — or somebody — lurks among the shrubs and watches with mild amusement the meanderings of visitors. After a prowl in the park you can believe in St. Francis of Assissi.

The house on the outside, as you can judge by the basic elements that have been used, is ungainly. But these are soon forgotten when you stand inside the tall staircase hall, which is the forerunner of an idea used later by Wyatt in his scheme for Ashridge. Above you, at first floor level, there are clusters of Gothic shafts which don't detract from the spectacular staircase. This construction rises in one flight and then divides into two separate flights like a bird stretching its wings. Here's one answer to the cramped lifts in modern buildings.

The rest of the interior of the house is a decorator's delight since Lord Sheffield — whatever his shortcomings — clearly preferred classical detail to live with and one must assume that the Gothic exterior was dictated by a limited budget. There's a frieze with sphinxes and lions in elliptical medallions and a fine stucco ceiling in the style of Adams. This, however, is surpassed by the drawing room where the corners have fan motifs — an echo of Gothic — and the cove is a jungle of lions, tigers and cheetahs. These, like the segmental ceiling, were painted by Catton, a Royal Academician who was noted for his imaginative paintings of animals.

What was life like in Sheffield Park at the end of the 18th century and what type of man was Lord Sheffield? His family came originally from the West Riding of Yorkshire and John Baker Holroyd — who became Baron Sheffield in 1780 and later Lord Sheffield — was a man of many talents that included the ability to write lucidly and speak well in the political field. He had a sound knowledge of business and was a skilful administrator. He was M.P. for Coventry, commanded a regiment of Light Dragoons and earned a peerage. At this period in his life he enlarged and rebuilt Sheffield Park.

In the portrait exhibited in the Royal Academy in 1806, and in Sir Joshua Reynolds' pencil drawing, you can see why women were attracted by his looks and why men, like Gibbon, valued his friendship. Lord Sheffield married three times. His first wife died in 1793, after bearing three children of which two girls survived, and he remarried a year later on Boxing Day 1794. His second wife, Lady Lucy Pelham, was the daughter of the Earl of Chichester, a fragile little thing who only lived in Sheffield Place as Lady Sheffield for three years before she died in 1797.

Perhaps the political scheming and the entertaining that was necessary in country houses was an exhausting business? There was little opportunity for a private life and quiet pursuits when you were a public figure in the 18th century and it needed someone with the stamina of the third Lady Sheffield to bear a son and heir as well as acting as hostess, mistress and ministering angel. Her marriage in 1798, a year after the death of the second Lady Sheffield, was a test of left-handed human endeavour.

Lord Sheffield had been instrumental in establishing the Lewes Wool Fair (in 1780) where the prices of wool were fixed. He presided at the meetings when he wasn't dashing up to Downing Street and was, I suspect, a blunt man whose tenacity and prolific writing left others — less strong and less talented — exhausted. His unromantic tomb for Gibbon in the Sheffield Mausoleum — just a name engraved in marble — would indicate a man who was too busy to bother about trimmings when they were unnecessary. But Gibbon has left us a clear assessment of Lord Sheffield's charm in the words: "His hospitable kindness and the most pleasant period was that which I passed in the domestic society of his family."

Happiness, it seems, could be found at Sheffield Place, the halfway house between too little and too much.

GOODWOOD HOUSE. 4½ miles north east of Chichester between the A 285 and the A 286. Owned by the Goodwood Estate Company.

When I used to complain to my grandfather on the subject of my resemblance to a beanpole he merely patted my head, if he could find it, and commented: "Whoever heard of a fat thoroughbred?" Many people associate the name of Goodwood with racing, which has taken place there for 170 years. The 3rd Duke of Richmond laid out the course on a fine site, high on the Sussex Downs, and the first meeting was held in 1801 on Trundle Hill. Stubbs, the painter, stayed at Goodwood early in his life and painted racehorses in training being watched by the 3rd Duke and his Duchess.

In Goodwood Park, 60 acres of woodland and grassland, there are noble avenues of chestnuts and beech trees. Here, on the southern slopes of the Downs, the views across the coastal plain are amongst the finest in Sussex. The cedars of Lebannon, 18th century planting, have grown until some measure 25 feet round the trunk. There are 30 different types of oak tree and a romantic old windmill at Halnaker which was a ruin until it was restored by Sir William Bird as a memorial to his wife. The Goodwood Estate covers 12,000 acres and my aunt, a plump local landmark, claims to be the only one the estate doesn't own.

There's an abundance of natural beauty at Goodwood. So much, in fact, that one wonders whether nature — conscious of the hazards of men who in the name of progress erode the landscape — laid in such a mighty stock that it defied extinction? You catch sight of Goodwood House when you descend from the racecourse and it is a building that was designed from the outset as a home for a family. And a home it has remained for the families of the Dukes of Richmond and Gordon and the Gordon Lennox family. The house dates back to the 12th century but for the period before the 18th century it was used as a Hunting Seat. The 3rd Duke of Richmond instigated the building of Martello Towers to forestall the invasion of our coastline by Napoleon. He was also responsible for Goodwood House as it stands today. Sir William Chambers was the architect who designed the elegant Stables' block near the end of the 1750s and, in 1760, he was instructed to rebuild the house. The centre of the present building — the Long Hall — appears to be his work. But in the years 1790 to 1800, the Duke of Richmond decided to build a more suitable house for his way of living and commissioned James Wyatt to build an opulent octagon with towers at the angles.

But to be an aristocrat in art you have to avoid the cost of polite society and, unfortunately, the Duke's funds were not sufficient to build the type of grandiose house he had evisaged. Nonplussed, he settled for a scheme that surrounded the old house by new building and the old Hunting Seat of 1720 — a plain brick building with skimped stone dressings — is contained within the three sides of the octagon that were completed. The Duke, probably as an economy, specified the use of flint and stone which, although a bit dull in combination, have left us with one of the finest examples of Sussex flintwork. Petworth Road was also re-routed so that the views from the windows were improved. The Kennels, built in 1787, were lavish even for a hunting fanatic and prompted John Kent to write: "No such buildings for the comfort and occupation of dogs were to be seen elsewhere."

Inside Goodwood House the rooms are not particularly noteworthy architecturally. The style seems to suggest that either Wyatt was limited by finance or had lost heart. The Long Hall, however, was the core of the original Jacobean House planned in 1729, designed by Sir William Chambers. Renovations have brought to light the original chimneys. The drawing-room — now known as the Tapestry Drawing Room — was once rebuilt by Chambers and redesigned by Wyatt to show off the tapestries acquired by the 3rd Duke when he was Ambassador in Paris in 1765. In one of the towers you'll discover the Card Room, one of the most pleasing rooms in the house. The decoration in this room is light and delicate which echoes the effect achieved in the Shell Grotto. The Card Room contains Sèvres porcelain, furniture veneered with a kingwood marquetry and a circular carpet that reveals the skills that made Axminster famous in the early years. The purpose of the room reminds me of the remark: "A great social success is a pretty girl who plays her cards carefully as if she were plain."

Goodwood House has sufficient atmosphere and treasures to compensate for any lack of style. The Dukes who lived there have each contributed something relative to the history of their times. My own favourite was Sarah, Duchess of Richmond, wife of the Second Duke, who built with her daughters the Shell House, a grotto lined with shells sent to the family in the 1740s by Captain Knowles of HMS Diamond and other officers. The task took seven years to complete and the result is a delicate essay in perseverance and period charm. It is an enduring personal contribution to the family estate. The shells remind one of the chrysanthemums, described by Edith Sitwell as " art shades of mauve, and terracotta and russet, smell of moths, camphorball, and drowned sailors."

The paintings, perhaps, reflect the most exciting aspect of a united family continuing their purpose of creating a home worthy of public inspection and private pleasure. The Ballroom, designed by the 3rd Duke to double as a gallery, has splendid portraits by Van Dyck, the court painter, Lely and Kneller. In the Main Entrance Hall there are two London views by Canaletto and, in the Long Hall, three famous pictures by Stubbs as well as some of the fine sporting paintings commissioned by the 2nd Duke. Gobelin tapestries hang in the Drawing Room and in the Blue Hall you can see George Smith's painting of the Grotto. It's a rich feast, confirming that we build for our needs and sacrifice our pockets to art.

The Dukes of Richmond and Gordon, like the coral building a barrier reef against the sea, made their own barriers against the tide of change by crowding their home and their lives with aspects of pleasure. We can learn a lot from them today when the wind of change blows even harder.

PARHAM, PULBOROUGH.   2 miles west of Storrington on the A 283.

When you view the setting of some old houses the dream decays and the props crumble. I've always seen Parham as the perfect Tudor house in the perfect Tudor landscape, where trees and ferns are emphasised instead of being flattened in the manner of 18th century landscaping. At Pulborough, the downland setting is beautiful and the house sits naturally in the parkland, 500 acres of it, flanked by the little church that seems to be keeping the stately mansion company.

There's an atmosphere about Parham which suggests a coquette that rouses passions she has no intention of gratifying. Fortunately, one *is* gratified because the house is not an Elizabethan extravagance like Danny House at Hurstpierpoint. Even the 20th century restorations have been carried out with an understanding of 16th century principles. The house was originally built by Sir Thomas Palmer and the foundation stone of the E shaped building is dated January 1577. You can also read the lines which Byron wrote of Lady Wilmot Horton when he was desperately trying to prove that he was a true womaniser beyond hint of homosexuality: " She walks in beauty like the night." His lines are in Parham and might equally have applied to the deer and herons that have been on the estate for centuries. The cedars have also been on the estate for centuries and the large plane trees by the church. There are avenues, vistas, lily ponds and a terrace by the lake where the mists rise like summer ghosts.

Parham was once a grange of Westminster Abbey and probably the four centred arches in the north west corners were a kitchen. If you stand in the doorway of the church you can realise that the stone faced house, with its large grids of mullioned windows giving an impression of lightness, expresses the Elizabethan delight in picturesque regularity. The spirit of that age speaks for itself in architecture as fine as this. Inside the house, the hall and gallery are notable but some rooms were decorated in the 18th century. The chapel, like the church, has a unique font. This is made of wood, carved with representations of Adam and Eve. It's the only one of this type in Sussex and even the serpent seems to be saying: " Why not?" The church font is one of three lead fonts in Sussex and was made in 1351 with a decoration of heraldry that includes the arms of Andrew Peverell.

Parham was built for the lord of the manor and the main facade faces south. This was unusual because the Tudors feared diseases being encouraged by this aspect. An Elizabethan Hall was always entered from the centre of the south front and the rest of the planning developed round this feature. The Great Hall at Parham has a steward's room above instead of a gallery and the fortunate man had an ideal position for viewing the hall through two wooden mullioned openings which supported the timber framing overhead. The Long Gallery is pure 16th century but the roof is 19th century work. The Gallery was planned to suit the kind of life that was led at Parham, and provided an up and down walk with side to side views. This was, of course, before anybody had had a few goblets of Malmsey.

The main staircase, planned behind the high table end of the hall, was built round a core of solid masonry. This was functional. The Great Chamber and the 18th century salon are simple rooms, also functional, designed to suit their uses. The rooms contain many unique and beautiful furnishings, needlework and portraits which are Elizabethan, Jacobean and Georgian. The portrait of Elizabeth the First is attributed to Zucchero and so is the portrait of Robert Dudley, Earl of Leicester. The portrait of Lady Frederick Campbell was painted by Gainsborough and the portrait of Mary Curzon, governess to the children of Charles Stuart, was painted by Van Dyck. Both sitters and painters now entertain the most exclusive worms.

Robert Palmer owned Parham before his son, Thomas Palmer, started work on the building existing today. That was in 1577. Twenty years later, Thomas Palmer's son, another Thomas, sold Parham to Thomas Bisshopp of Henfield. It is believed that Queen Elizabeth, on one of her indefatiguable journeys, stayed at Parham which raises the question: "How many beds other than her own did she *really* sleep in?" My own guess is that she probably dined there with the Palmer family so that the ladies who accompanied her could rest. Ladies, in those days, were people who did not do things for themselves.

By 1815, the house belonged to Lord Zouche and remained in the family through the century. The history of the house is a long one, dating back to the days before the Norman Conquest when the land was owned by a free man called Tovi. Strangely, this fine Elizabethan House seems to have remained aloof to the occupants and has made its own history by retaining within the bricks and mortar an expression of a way of life dictated by a way of living. Perhaps the grandeur of Parham has been too great for the owners to match in the scale of their private lives? Elizabeth the First remained a Queen in her own room with the door shut. The same is true of Parham.

In the little church of St. Peter's there's an enviable record of one local man who lived from the time of Charles the First through to the reign of George the First. He had six wives, three of whom he married in one century and the remainder in the second century. He may have modelled his life on Henry the Eighth's and lost his heart as frequently as his wives lost their heads.

13. Theatres of Sussex. Stage by Stage

When the curtain rises on a stage today, belief is suspended in the same way that it was at the time of Greek theatre, when actors wore masks designed to express emotions for them and voices had to give meaning to the verse. Many people wear masks without being on the stage and I agree with Augustus William Hare's words: " Everybody has his own theatre, in which he is manager, actor, prompter, playwright, sceneshifter, boxkeeper, doorkeeper, all in one, and audience into the bargain ".

Thespis was a semi-legendary Greek dramatic poet of the 6th century and actors, classified as Thespians, have usually received appreciative applause from theatre-lovers in Sussex. There aren't many theatres in the county, but what we have are choice. So, too, are Sussex-born actors, like Paul Schofield, and there are many who are Sussex by adoption. Kemp Town, in Brighton, is home for a small colony of actors which includes Laurence Olivier and his wife, Joan Plowright. The unforgettable production of *Uncle Vanya*, during the opening season at the Chichester Festival Theatre, owed a great deal to the performances of the Oliviers and set the seal on the theatre's success that season.

Lord Olivier was also the theatre's first director until 1966, when Sir John Clements was invited to become director. Sir John, during his first year, scored a personal stage success as the General in Anouilh's comedy *The Fighting Cocks*. The first stage of the Chichester Festival Theatre was built in 1962 after a successful campaign had been launched to raise funds. Architects Powell and Moya, with an associate architect Christopher Stevens, designed an open thrust stage with 1,360 seats in one tier for the six sided auditorium, where each seat is within 66 feet of the stage. The stage balcony could be removed to allow for a variation of setting and the final cost, £178,300, was modest by standards then current. The cost of theatre building is rising each year and has overtaken most managements. In 1966, when Sir John Clements became director, the foyer was extended to improve the cramped, limited backstage facilities and to allow the public to breath during the interval. Prior to this improvement, the rush for the bar had been like finding oneself caught up in an unexpected riot in Hyde Park.

Stage two of the development was made possible by further donations to the 1000 Club, patrons of the theatre at Chichester, but the theatre had paid its own way from money taken at the new box office, donated by the Arts Council of Great Britain, who must have been grateful to help a theatre that could support itself without begging for aid. Plays by modern playwrights, which included Peter Shaeffer's *Royal Hunt Of The Sun* and *Black Comedy*, have been successfully combined in seasons with plays by Shakespeare, Shaw and Strindberg. Robert Bolt's *Vivat! Vivat! Regina*, with his wife Sarah Miles and Eileen Atkins, was praised but, for me, the production of *Othello* with Laurence Olivier, gravel-voiced as the Moor, Frank Finlay as Iago and Maggie Smith as Desdemona has yet to be equalled as a memorable theatre event. Each season at Chichester has had star quality. The imposing list of actors that have appeared on the open stage include Sir John Gielgud, Sir Michael Redgrave, Topol, Laurence Harvey, Nigel Patrick, Albert Finney, Robert Stephens and three Dames, Sybil Thorndyke, Edith Evans and Margaret Rutherford. Actresses who have attracted full houses include Joan Plowright, Margaret Leighton, Celia Johnson, Margaret Johnston, Joan Greenwood, Fenella Fielding, Irene Handl, Beatrice Lehmann, Billie Whitelaw, Dora Bryan, Irene Worth and Anna Calder Marshall. A visiting Canadian Company, from Stratford, Ontario, gave full-blooded Shakespearian performances in their production of *Timon Of Athens*. The theatre is at Oaklands Park and has its own restaurant where Danish Smorrebrod is served, to 160 people in 20 minutes when necessary. Concentration, when eating, is the key to getting back to your seat in time for the second half of the play.

The drama season at the Chichester Festival Theatre is from May to September and there are concerts during the winter. The De La Warr Pavilion at Bexhill has symphony concerts during the winter, a festival of classical music during the summer and a festival of light music during the autumn. This is excellent for those people whose musical experiences are limited to two a year and bridges the gap between Ivor Novello and Mozart for them. You don't have to run to the hills for the sound of music at Bexhill where Erich Mendelsohn and Serge Chermayeff, whose names sound like distinguished musicians to me, built the De La Warr Pavilion between 1933 and 1936. The concrete building is a clean-cut piece of modern architecture facing the sea, with a well glazed staircase for the short-sighted and, as a focal point on the seafront, the design makes most of the surrounding buildings look seasick. Another Pavilion, The White Rock Pavilion at Hastings, has a music festival in March, when the wind blows inside and outside, and a summer show suitable for families for whom the theatre is a holiday event, like pantomime. Jack Tripp, the comedian, cut his teeth in summer shows like The Fol-De-Rols. His own shows at Hastings, as well as appearances in pantomime, have recaptured a lost art in the profession, the ability to raise laughter from your audiences with clean material. Marie Lloyd had other views.

Bexhill started as a resort thirty years later than Eastbourne, which was established in 1850. Both resorts have seaside development, often buildings that show the weariness of age and the sadness of decline. Both places have old centres, away from the sea, although Eastbourne's parts which were separate originally, Senhouses, Meades, Bourne and East Bourne, have become united over the years. The Seventh Duke of Devonshire was responsible for progressive development in 1851 and the Devonshire Park Theatre, in the recreation ground grandly titled Devonshire Park, was built with two Italianate towers in 1884. The theatre now has all year round repertory which, in my experience, invariably has the effect of making sedate actors transform themselves into smiling, tousle-haired juvenile leads of appalling winsomeness. "Acting with one of them," an actress has said, "is like acting with two tons of condemned veal."

Eastbourne, fortunately, has a civic, multi-purpose hall theatre, with 1,678 seats in two tiers, which was built in 1963 on the edge of Devonshire Park. The Congress Theatre was designed by architects B. and N. Westwood, Piet and Partners and is interesting for the way in which the conventional auditorium can be adapted to suit the wide variety of functions that some seaside theatres have to provide. The reinforced concrete structure was faced with grey-blue bricks and white slabs, which are pleasantly restrained. The materials also give a clean and crisp appearance to the theatre, which replaced the Winter Garden that had been on the site since 1874. The Congress Theatre has three assembly halls of various sizes and the foyer bars are sufficiently generous in size to prevent congestion during intervals, which is a relief. The glazed galleries provide plenty of crush space area unlike some in Sussex where the conversation doesn't flow with the drink but drowns in it. The auditorium converts into a conventional stage-orientated theatre by the use of black Venetian blinds and the area can be decreased to seat only 600, when there are meetings and lectures, by curtaining that reduces the volume. A restaurant links the theatre entrance foyer and the existing Winter Gardens, a collision that is not a happy one, although the restaurant overlooks the park and is a comfortable place to air your particular theatre hobby horse, a vehicle once used by the 19th century dandies in Sussex.

The play must go on because, as most actors will confirm, if there's no play then there's no pay. The Connaught Theatre, at Worthing, has created stars from the repertory companies, changing tribes of actors, that have performed in the town. The Saxon name ending *-ing* — meant belonging to a tribe, in Worthing's history meant Wurp's People. Peggy Mount appeared in *Sailor Beware*, by Philip King, at Worthing and, despite her versatility, the public wanted her as Ma Hornet, that monstrous mother-in-law, and never as Topsy. But, like Topsy, the ballet school turned theatre, to which Dame Adeline Genée lent her name, grew and grew in a gentle sloping field, surrounded by pine trees, in East Grinstead. The opening was in January 1967, a Royal Gala Performance, finally backed by adequate funds to ensure that the initial shell was equipped with 330 seats, ideal lighting and accommodation that included a stage deep enough for ballet, a workshop, Green Room and dressing rooms. The scheme, for those connected with its growth, was a labour of love. They may have taken comfort from Arthur Wing Pinero's words: "Those who love deeply never grow old. They may die young, but they never grow old."

Youth is sometimes portrayed on the stage as inarticulate, pimply and lovesick. The Gardner Centre for the Arts, at the University of Sussex, is sited in Stanmer Park, former home of the Earls of Chichester. The Centre owes a great deal of its success to the vitality and support of youth. The design evolved from the idea of uniting the arts in a single building, circular in plan, with surrounding studios for music, painting and sculpture for students and the " artists in residence " to use. Sean Kenny was the theatre consultant to the architects. The Gardner Centre has the rare distinction in Sussex of providing a building where music, opera, ballet, folk singers, drama and exhibitions of paintings can be accommodated by adapting the internal fittings. The swivel seats, for audiences up to 500, can be rearranged within the auditorium but there are no cushions and the effect, on me, reduces the pleasure of the entertainment to rock bottom. The shallow open platform, 60 feet deep, is not always suitable for staging plays which require an atmosphere of enclosure for their full effect. *The Doll's House*, when it was staged at the Gardner Centre with Fenella Fielding, was robbed of its impact on the open stage. But when jazz, folk and chamber music are performed, the stage establishes an excellent rapport between performers and audience. The bar, near the art gallery, encourages people to mix and talk together but the intimacy achieved by the limited space is offset by the free-for-all that occurs when coffee, coats and campari have to be manipulated. You just have to take a deep breath and enjoy the chaotic freemasonry.

The comfort and convenience of audiences has not always been paramount in the design of modern theatres, which are challenging and complicated buildings for architects. You don't expect comfort in end-of-pier theatres and it's a pleasant surprise if you are comfortable during a Summer Show after the bracing walk out to sea. On a windy day, you might find yourself in it. If I praise the Theatre Royal at Brighton highly it's because the theatre has style, comfort and character. The walls, historical though they are, don't bear the heavy burden of gilt that can be as untheatrical as a tiara without gems. The standard of plays has always been a high one in my experience, and the atmosphere, as well as the audiences, has encouraged many leading actors to perform there. Acting is an interpretive art and those who have failed at the Theatre Royal have had an affinity with the work of Madame Tussaud, whose name has been identified with wax since the 19th century. Their performances have been lifeless.

The Theatre Royal at Brighton is in New Road, named during Regency times after New Street which it replaced. The road was built by soldiers and the new theatre, built in 1806, replaced the old theatre in Duke Street when it became inadequate for holding the increasing number of visitors to the town. The bow windows and colonnade, both elegant features, of the Theatre Royal were additions of 1826. The theatre opened in June, 1807, under the Prince Regent's patronage when Mr. and Mrs. Charles Kemble appeared as Hamlet and Ophelia. The building had cost £12,000 to construct, with equipment included, and the early managements experienced difficulties with the rent. They also had to meet the high cost of paying stars and mounting expensive productions to satisfy the sophisticated tastes of Brighton audiences. Grimaldi, Edmund and Charles Kean, Madame Vestris and Sarah Siddons are among the great names of the stage that have appeared on old playbills. The Theatre Royal was remodelled between 1885 and 1894 when the red brick and terracotta frontage was built. The Ionic capped columns, plump at the base like Calabash pears, were also of that period.

Other famous actors and actresses that have appeared on the stage in Brighton include Ellen Terry, Sarah Bernhardt, Julia

Neilson, Martin Harvey, Henry Irving, Seymour Hicks, Weedon Grossmith and Fred Terry. Mrs. Patrick Campbell also acted at the Theatre Royal, where the surfeit of admirers may have prompted her to say: " Marriage is the result of longing for the deep, deep peace of the double-bed after the hurly-burly of the chaise-longue." Today's stars continue the tradition of fine acting in first productions for which the theatre is noted. My friend, J. Baxter Somerville, managed the theatre from 1937 to the end of his life in 1963. The success of the theatre in those years was due to his enthusiasm and encouragement for the staff and the stars. Theatre management can be compared to a building facade which, if it is poorly constructed, will crumble and reveal that there is nothing behind it.

Sussex is fortunate in having theatres which have survived from the past or have been created, in recent years, by people with a strong desire to continue the tradition of first rate entertainment in the county. The lyric in the musical play, *Me and Juliet,* sums up one attitude to the theatre: " While actors keep acting, and plays keep attracting, the theatre will never be dead." Theatres, if they are to survive in the future, should avoid the fate of an 18th century actress, who took a new lover every year and invariably became pregnant. " She's like certain European nations," remarked Sophie Arnould of the Opéra Comique, " always extending her frontiers, but never retaining her conquests."

The Lanes at Brighton
originally pathways defining gardens when the 18th Century fishermen's
cottages formed the village of Brighthelmstone.

Brunswick Square, Hove
a classic example of elegant seaside architecture
in Regency days

Regency seaside house at Brighton
as cheerful in its design as a summer's day
when the sun shines.
(Reproduced by courtesy of the Brighton Herald Ltd.)

14. Follies and Fantasies.
Eyecatchers in the Rye

Most of us have suffered from follies of our own making but only a fortunate few of us have enjoyed building them. Buildings which are foolishly-conceived cannot always be classified as follies for the builders of follies invariably built for amusement and pleasure. They have been designed in past centuries by Nash, Vanbrugh and Chute. The impulses that inspired Mad Jack Fuller and the Duchess of Richmond were the same as those which today inspire crackpot aunts, aided by an au pair, to build a sham castle with shards.

The name and nature of the folly defies analysis, but they represent the ideas and sentiments that have driven their creators to give them solid and permanent form. Many, therefore,have been carefully preserved particularly when they have been built on property now owned by the National Trust. Those that continue their life as picturesque ruins, like myself, enhance a prospect if nothing else. The present day equivalent of the 18th century follies, which combine pleasing decay and picturesque settings in Sussex, are — in part — buildings for amusement. In these, the elements of fantasy and sensation, needed by people who find the world of reality maddening, offer relaxation and an antidote to tensions. Romantic melancholy inspired writers and folly builders in the past. Lack of it inspires them today.

Follies were built from the late 16th century to the early 20th century but, during the 18th century when the Gothic mood crept in, men and women of wealth built for pleasure. The inspiration for many ideas derive from the pattern books of the period, particularly Batty Langley's *Gothic Architecture by Rules and Proportions in Many Grand Designs* (1742) and William Wrighte's *Grotesque Architecture or Rural Amusement* (1767). In the 18th and 19th centuries a folly added ornament to a gentleman's estate and many amateurs, afflicted by artistic temperament, set about building a surfeit of castellated

abbeys, monumental tombs and Gothic towers for owls to haunt.
You could judge a man's wealth by his ruin.

The structures were frequently built of fragile materials,
wood and canvas frames with a cement coating, to achieve
maximum effect at minimum expense. Those that exist in
Sussex today seem to have been built of sturdy materials like
brick and flint and, despite the fact that they were follies, their
owners seemed determined that they should last. Grottoes, too,
still exist in Sussex and there is a particularly fine example at
Goodwood which illustrates the ingenious use of shells in an
artificially created setting. Unfortunately, they lack the legends
that are associated with follies. But grottoes are old hat today
despite the fact that they were once built by families who
disliked towns and were rich enough to inhabit counties.
Follies and grottoes were fun to build and were never intended
to express a serious message. If the intentions of their
architects had been serious, then probably everybody would
have thought of them as a joke.

The stone minarets on the Royal Pavilion, the marine folly in
Brighton, originally weighed 40 tons each when John Nash, the
architect, designed them. Today they are being replaced by
fibre glass copies which weigh about 8 hundredweight. The
wheel has turned full circle. Fantasy architecture, like the
Royal Pavilion, is not always superficial and each century has
contributed a coup de thêatre to enliven the scene. Eye-catch-
ing follies of the past in Sussex have survived the growth of ivy
and the criticism that they were symptoms of insanity. They
were invariably built by men of intelligence and humourous
nature in times of peace and prosperity. The roof shapes on the
Royal Pavilion were designed for their effect in silhouette, one
of the considerations to surprise strangers who stumbled across
a folly.

Sussex is fortunate to have benefited from the indulgences of
Mad Jack Fuller. In his more serious moments, he was
responsible for the preservation of Bodiam Castle and saved
this spectacular piece of moated architecture from death by a
thousand indecisions. You don't have to live half your life in a
cemetery to be vehement about historical preservation. John
Fuller was wealthy and unmarried, probably realising that
there is no escape from an affectionate woman. He was a large
man, over 20 stone in weight and affectionately nicknamed
" Hippo ", lucky enough to possess a cheerful and benevolent
nature. He owned Rose Hill in the early 19th century before it
became Brightling Park and when he was fifty he fell victim to
the fever that afflicts folly builders. Before he started, he gave
the local church of St. Thomas a' Becket a splendid barrel

organ which one can only assume was a peace offering before his spree of mischievious building. His contributions to the follies of Sussex were simple and unsubtle revealing a clarity of architectural perception that would appear to have started with the bottle. He lived to be 77, however, and died in 1834 having built follies that included a cone, a pyramid, a tomb, an obelisk, an observatory and a hermit's tower at Dallington and Brightling from 1810 onwards. These could all be described as back-slapping gestures.

The cone — The Sugar Loaf — is made of stone and cement. The folly was intended to represent the steeple of Dallington Church, which Mad Jack had sworn could be seen from his dining room. The drunken dinner table boast had to be substantiated when, the morning after the night before, he discovered that there was no steeple in view. He therefore set about building his cone, 40 feet high, a folly that became functional when it was used as a cottage earlier this century. Robert Smirke was responsible for the designs of the Observatory and Rotunda which were added to the Fuller land. Mad Jack designed the Brightling Needle, which stands 650 feet above sea level to the west of the church, as a landmark close to the four-square Observatory. The Observatory, like The Sugar Loaf, became a house eventually and is used as such today.

Mad Jack also built his own mausoleum, a pyramid shaped tomb, 24 years in advance of his death. He was probably chuckling at the time when he added yet another folly to the mare's nests he had already created. No hermit ever lived in the hermit's tower he built, but the genial gentleman was larger than life and even allowed walls to be built round his park to keep the unemployed occupied in times of hardship. I like to believe the legend that he was discovered sitting in his tomb, fully dressed, enjoying a large meal and several bottles of wine. You can imagine him saying: " Eat, drink and be merry for tomorrow we won't die." He was a man as big-hearted as the jokes he has left us.

There are other follies in Sussex, splendid examples of 18th century idiosyncracies or symbols of ennui depending on how you view them. The Marquis of Abergavenny's estate at Eridge has a brick prospect tower, 600 feet high, on Saxonbury Hill. This folly, built in 1820, is well hidden by the woods on the hilltop where an Iron Age hill fort was discovered in the early 20th century. Another tower, this time at Heathfield, was built by Francis Newbury in 1793 as a tribute to Lord Heathfield who, as General Elliott, defended Gibraltar during the Franco-Spanish siege of 1779. Gibraltar Tower, a landmark on the

Weald, was partly destroyed by fire but the lower octagonal part still remains. You can find Jack Cade's stone — a memorial to the leader of the Kentish Rebellion — to the north of the old village. Near Toat Farm, Pulborough, there is a six sided tower built about 1823 in memory of Samuel Drinkald on the spot where he died when his horse threw him. The folly, known as Toat Memorial, has given rise to a spate of legends that seem to haunt these quaint buildings that enliven the countryside.

At Uppark you'll find a red brick tower, once cemented, that was built in the 1770s as a 21st birthday present for Sir Henry Featherstonhaugh. The folly, Featherstonhaugh Tower, has become a bit seedy with age and decay has quietly removed the traceried windows and pinnacles that were once part of the design. Emma Hamilton is reputed to have flitted round it, presumably chased by Lord Nelson, while other stories assure you that the Prince Regent used the park as a happy hunting ground when he wanted to lay his lady prey. They must all have been splendid runners, if the stories carry any truth, because the park is vast.

Lord Gage is said to have signalled messages to his deer-keeper at Ringmer, 7 miles away from Firle Tower on the Gage Estate. The folly, which is circular and castellated, was built at the foot of the South Downs, West Firle, in 1822 and is a pleasant piece of whimsy. The same thing cannot be said about Nore Folly at Slindon, built in the late 18th century as a luncheon room, after hunts, for the Earl of Newburgh. The Gothic arch shape was well suited to the needs of the railway authorities when they needed a tunnel entrance. The flint columns, walls, arches and machiolations were sturdy enough to withstand vibrations although the shooting parties the folly once served would not, I feel, have approved.

The handsome folly at Clayton — the tunnel entrance — was built in 1840. The detail is Gothic and the basic idea was to provide a house for the tunnel keeper and his family. Their compensation for noise, soot and shaking walls in this brick pied-à-terre near Hassocks was to have the house set between turrets, machiolations and battlements in order, I assume, to make the family feel invincible. The walls and furniture may vibrate madly but Clayton Tunnel carries on, as jokey a folly as you'll find in any other county.

Racton tower, near Rowlands Castle, Racton, is for nature lovers who enjoy views and fine trees. The brick and flint tower was built in 1770 and today, eroded but still standing, it is only 75 feet high. The triangular plan once had four towers but three of them have fallen prey to the effects of nature and vandalism. This was once a glorious folly, five floors high and extremely well designed judging by the brick vaulting, the round arched windows and the small remains of mouldings and plasterwork. The original cost was £10,000 and Lord Halifax, for whom it was built, must have enjoyed looking towards Chichester harbour and firing salutes from the tower top like a frustrated general.

Perhaps Lord Halifax shared the views of Sarah, wife of the Second Duke of Richmond, who completed the Shell Grotto in Goodwood Park in the 1740s with the help of her daughters. After seven years hard work on this delicate and rheumatism encouraging task she was still able to say: " It will be the legitimate butt of all sophisticated mockery. But it was built for pleasure as others will discover."

15. Pubs & Eating Places.
Inns and Outs

In a Sussex restaurant recently I was told that "for connoisseurs of good food the chef was prepared to cook anything not on the menu". This made sense, in a mad sort of way, after a glance at the plates of the people eating at a neighbouring table.

There have always been chew and choke restaurants in the county, to act as reminders of our Saxon heritage. There are also others which are a gourmet's paradise. George the Fourth, when faced with a political crisis, retired to bed to be bled by leeches and to gnaw cold chicken or gobble game pie. Nash, Chippendale, Byron, Shelley, Keats, Nelson, Wellington, Peel, and even Mrs. Fitzherbert (the original Fatso) all had notable appetites. Egon Ronay, Clement Freud and Cyril Ray are today's crusaders against wine and food which are not the crème de la crème. You cannot expect champagne for the price of Vichy water but you can always keep trying.

Wining and dining in Sussex can be a rewarding pastime particularly when you discover a small restaurant of character, or an inn off the beaten track, before other people converge on it like vultures. You can find great satisfaction in first class hotels and internal agony in some with no stars. Eating out in Sussex, as in any other part of the country, can be an adventure or a disaster. If you do have the misfortune to dine in a quaint old Sussex farmhouse where the main course tastes like cattle fodder then you can only shrug your shoulders and take

comfort from the words of N. F. Simpson in his play, The Hole;
" I eat merely to put food out of my mind."

The advantages of dining and drinking places in Sussex are
that the best have an historical background worth discovering
and imposing menus backed by well-stocked wine cellars.
Sussex pubs, nowadays, can offer excellent meals in up-to-date
dining rooms — The Wine Lodge at Worthing is a good example
— and there are several manor houses, like Slaugham Manor
Hotel, Handcross, which have the elegance of fine buildings
combined with 20th century comfort. The grounds are pleasant
places to walk round when you want fresh air to help you
recover from the shock of the bill. Meals that start in a light
vein can easily become varicose when insufficient care has been
given to the preparation and serving of food. Lavender Cottage
at Bramber does a great deal to restore one's faith in hospitable
restaurateurs who carry on even when the chef has passed out
from garlic fumes. You'll be cossetted, too, at The Hungry
Monk, Jevington and also at The Bolney Stage, Bolney.

Insignificant entrances should never deter the determined
and the knowledgeable. This is sometimes a subtle ploy to
maintain a regular and faithful clientele. La Mer at Peacehaven is usually fully booked; table space is limited and there
is virtually no room for further reservations. This also applies
to restaurants in Chichester during the season of plays at the
Festival Theatre and they still seem fully booked when the
season ends. Places where the food is considered more
important then the surroundings usually have a devoted
following as well as being well planned and comfortable. The
pub which flows naturally into a dining area, like the Pelham
Arms at Lewes, has the added advantage of enabling you to eat
while others drink. You may have to eat in public like the
royal courts of France. Marie Antoinette, when asked if this
embarassed her remarked " We eat quickly."

One man's restaurant can be another man's poison, and this
is equally true of pubs which please one taste and are anathema
to another. Restaurants and pubs in Sussex can be found in
converted cottages and houses, original village inns that now
cater for coaches and motorists instead of cart owners and
carriages. There are books which carry an impressive selection
of pubs and eating places, particularly *Sussex Pubs* by Rodney
L. Walkerley and Egon Ronay's *Good Food Guide*. Vegetarians
are catered for in many towns, and Ceres Health Food
Restaurants will satisfy those intent on slimming. If you must
slim, eat as much as you like but don't swallow it.

The following selection of restaurants are in Brighton, often
called London-By-The-Sea, where the variety in types of eating

places seems higher than elsewhere. Each town and resort in the county provides local people with a choice from which to select their own favourite place. My own list is a personal choice, based on years of indigestion and travelling with my food-taster. When you visit Brighton, as the world seems to do, I hope you will enjoy choosing from the polyglot menus — Chinese, French, Indian, Greek, Italian, Mexican, Swiss and Forte. The Austrians don't seem to have discovered a potential market in Brighton yet, although at a recent food exhibition you could buy apple strudel. One purchaser returned to give her views. " I liked it immensely," she said, " but my husband and children complained. I can't think why, because I served it hot with fresh vegetables and a nice thick gravy."

There are six Chinese restaurants in Brighton and each offers its particular brand of oriental charm. THE CROWN OF JADE, in Ship Street, fulfils the eastern promise. You can neither approve anything so insular with regard to subdued lighting nor disapprove of anything so exotic. The black, gold and jade decor is Hong Kong modern and the service appears to be on wheels. Occasionally you might hear a short, sharp Chinese cry for freedom in the general direction of the kitchen but if you bury your head in the bar, or waltz gaily to records of Engelbert Humperdinck upstairs, you need not worry. The menu gives a clear indication of price and contents of dishes. The amount, however, is far larger than you anticipate and if the spare ribs are too filling then you can always let the Butter-fly Prawns take wing with the waiter or hide them in your napkin for the cat.

The Lanes in Brighton are a series of narrow alleys that were once part of medieval Brighthelmstone when it was a fishing village. It is not surprising, therefore, to find in this area a number of restaurants that serve only fish dishes. The Fishmarket on the seafront, where fish used to be unloaded and sold, was nearby. THE SHERIDAN TAVERN, in West Street, is an attractive place to be seen in and to see people you would like to know. A little snobbery never hurt anybody and you may catch a fleeting glimpse of Royalty in the green velvet dining room where the click of gold lighters drowns the sound of waiters, who announce their presence by the faint squeak of trolley wheels. The ephemeral is given lasting value. WHEELERS RESTAURANT, equally discreet, is in Market Street and if you trot through an adjacent twitten you'll find yourself outside ENGLISH'S OYSTER BAR, in East Street, where both walruses and carpenters rub shoulders. Here you may find remote and marine-like ladies snapping and gobbling up snippets of food between conversations. Fin and scale under floral dresses which, after cold ardour, would produce roe. But the true taste of Colchester and Whitstable can also be enjoyed in the smallest fish restaurant of all, D'ARCY'S in Market Street, where the owners do good by stealth and, to my delight, have it discovered by accident.

Brighton's four Indian restaurants are as simple in their decor as Gandhi's robes. THE TAJ MAHAL, in Ship Street, is a far cry from Agra but within shouting distance of the domes and minarets on the Royal Pavilion. THE MADRAS RESTAURANT, in Prince Albert Street, serves curries that are cool, medium and hair-raising. The aroma can be savoured in the street outside. The decorations inside are basic Bombay, with a picture of the Gods looking down hungrily. Expatriate Indians have found that their restaurants in Sussex often attract a curry-comb clientele as well as those with a taste for turmeric. Sir Winston Churchill, during his lifetime, said in the House of Commons: "The Almighty in His infinite wisdom did not see fit to create Frenchmen in the image of Englishmen." However, Frenchmen have discovered that the way to an Englishman's heart is through their cooking. Colonies of French inspired restaurants flourish throughout the county and the small stretch of English Channel that separates us from France has encouraged a steady exchange of tourists from both countries. Day trips, or longer holidays, from Newhaven to Dieppe are a particular summer pleasure but, when the weather is too formidable you can recapture the atmosphere briefly in Brighton at LE BISTRO, LE FRANCAIS, LA BELLE COCOTTE and AU PIED DU COCHON. THE TUREEN RESTAURANT, in Upper North Street, is French in spirit and English in price.

It is surprising that no cookery book has yet been published to record traditional Sussex recipes, although some dishes like Sussex Smokey, a compound of haddock, lemon juice and garlic, have a regional basis. We have yet to know the secrets contained in Framfield Tart, Golden Cross Chicken and Findon Haddock. Sussex restaurants excel in serving traditional food and their efforts are generally appreciated by those who prefer "no-nonsense cooking." These people don't look for a Maxim's in the middle of Midhurst but prefer to have their gastric juices stimulated by a well-made steak and kidney pudding in simple and comfortable surroundings. There are still hotels which have moved with the times, despite their Edwardian origins when men approved of everything except Father Christmas and votes for women. LANGFORDS, THE DUDLEY, THE QUEENS, THE GRAND, and THE METRO-POLE (where the Starlit Room is set on the top floor, defiantly modern) in Brighton respect the tradition for straightforward cooking and efficient waiter service. THE OLD SHIP was once a hotel where the Royal Mail Stagecoach pulled up on the seafront. Today, the building has been modernised and extended to welcome a different sort of transport but equally hungry travellers. This is also true of THE ROYAL ALBION, in The Steine, where earlier this century Sir Harry Preston held court with his bull terrier Sambo. The dog enjoyed a good steak and would, I think, have wagged his tail at those served in Brighton today at THE WAGON WHEEL STEAKHOUSE, Market Street, the SCOTCH STEAK HOUSE, West Street, the LONDON STEAK HOUSE, North Street and THE FOUR ACES in The Lanes.

The selection of Sussex pubs is based on their setting, atmosphere and hospitality and may encourage people to drive, or walk, over the Downs and far away to seek for themselves not only the places mentioned but also others, equally enjoyable, in the vicinity. The character of some pubs in the county has undergone brash modernisation which provokes one to call: "Drink to me only with thine eyes shut." A good pub is worth seeking out. A bad one makes you see double and feel single. A sense of fun is an absolute necessity if you want to keep your head in what are still local gathering places for villages. This also applies to certain pubs in towns. You're only young once, however, and after that you have to find excuses for what you've done in this absurdly short life.

There are three excellent pubs in Alfriston's one main street, behind which lies the church known as The Cathedral of the Downs because of its size. THE GEORGE, THE STAR and THE

MARKET CROSS are Sussex to the core, a trio with a surfeit of beams, designed in the days when people were shorter, and a cosy reminder of the times when stone roofs, leaded lights and mellow brickwork were made to last for centuries. THE GEORGE was a 14th century pull-up for pilgrims, THE MARKET CROSS was the haunt of smugglers and THE STAR has a Sanctuary Post to touch in the bar if you're on the run from justice. This is particularly appropriate in a Trust House hotel.

THE BLACK RABBIT is about half a mile from the centre of Arundel and faces the river bank where there are boat moorings. The pub dates back to the early 19th century when it was a popular stopping place for bargees and carriage trade. The old stables are now a restaurant and other alterations in recent years have provided visitors with a better view of the castle and surrounding countryside. The background is Rolls Royces and reeds. THE BRIDGE HOTEL, in Queen Street near Arundel Castle, is a Georgianised 20th century building where the work of local artists can be viewed through an impressionist haze. Nearby, in THE VICTORY, on the corner of Bond Street and King Street, you'll find echoes of the Battle of Trafalgar although the pub is a great deal older than early 19th century. The Nelson touch is everywhere but you can turn a blind eye to it and concentrate on what every publican expects you to do.

The National Trust owns Bodiam Castle, built in 1386, and also THE CASTLE INN, built early this century. The pub is robustly Edwardian (but now leased to the Arthur Guinness Company) with a generous car park in keeping with the portly customers who are redolent of brandy and cigars. The inn is an ideal stopping point for tourists exhausted by the roving journey round Battle Abbey, the heights of Hastings and the best of Bodiam. Tours of this kind often need a period of convalescence and one of the best places for this is Bognor Regis, where King George the Fifth found rest and peace in the countryside. There are two regal pubs, comfortable rather than notable, THE PRINCE OF WALES and THE SUSSEX HOTEL in the High Street. Those who are interested in fishing and golfing with find congenial company and an appreciative audience.

There are appreciative audiences every summer for the plays presented at Chichester's Festival Theatre. Chichester has a great deal to offer visitors in addition to the theatre, since history has provided the town with a natural backcloth. The pubs are part of the town's history and THE ROYAL ARMS, which is in East Street on a corner near the Market Cross, has a pedigree dating back to the 16th century when Queen

Elizabeth the First was entertained in the house then owned by Lord Lumley. The rich interior today has panelling dating back to that period, an Italian plaster ceiling equally old in the Elizabethan Room and bow windows that all provide the right atmosphere for actors to reminisce and businessmen to relax. South Street is part of the old city, with a quartet of pubs of which THE WHITE HORSE is one. Actors and businessmen also find the atmosphere of this 15th century place conducive to the pursuit of leisure, encouraged by the mellow qualities of the old oak beams and polished brass. THE KING'S HEAD, which once formed part of the property owned by the cathedral, has been privately owned since the end of the 18th century. The simple external elevation belies its history, which is firmly rooted in the 16th century. The service inside, however, is strictly 20th century. There are many show places in this city of fine pubs and in South Street you will also find THE GLOBE and THE FOUNTAIN, both comfortable places with surroundings that encourage drinking and being merry.

Everybody knows that there is no joy in drinking and driving, which may account for the reason why so many motorists spend so much time in pubs. Sussex can offer excellent village " locals " for the map-conscious scenery seekers although some of the public houses have been consciously smartened with paint and plush to attract the gin and tonic trade. THE FIVE BELLS at Chailey is Merrie England for Sunday motorists, who can enjoy the pleasures of log fires and log books. THE BULL, at Ditchling, is the oldest pub in the village where a drink will revive you after visiting Ditchling Beacon, the local landmark that has panoramic views. Feudal, rural and ethereal customers gather under the pub's antique oak beams which creak in sympathy. THE SHEPHERD AND DOG, at Fulking, is also a popular stop for motorists who have driven down into the hamlet that is dominated by the Devil's Dyke. There are no shepherds and no Southdown sheep to gaze on from the windows and the terrace of this cottage-style pub built in a hollow. There's a pleasant garden to wander round and you may find Maud in it after the black bat night has flown.

THE TIGER, East Dean, sits happily in the countryside between Eastbourne and Seaford. The pub faces a village green where wizened old gentlemen will regale you with their versions of the days of smugglers, wrecks off the coast and village cricket scores that would make W. G. Grace turn in his grave. Birling Gap, nearby, is on National Trust land and if you travel over Bullock Down, from which you can see Beachy Head lighthouse, you will be on the right road for Eastbourne, which is two miles away. Eastbourne has mainly modern pubs like THE PRINCE ALBERT, THE GILDREDGE and THE LION. You can see the sea from The Lion and all these places are ideal for a quiet, uneventful tipple with a lavender-scented aunt who will revel in the warmth, cleanliness and atmosphere of innocence. You receive the same courtesy when you order shandy or tomato juice as you do when you order a pint of black and tan. THE PILOT INN, in Meads Street, is pleasantly Victorian with a Smoke Room that doesn't prohibit aunts from smoking cheroots. Eastbourne is a pleasant place to visit. It has a genteel reputation dating back to the days when some ladies sported moustaches and elastic-sided boots.

The village of Rottingdean has a peaceful atmosphere similar to other small havens on the outskirts of large seaside resorts. THE WHITE HORSE INN takes its name from the horse owned by the King of Prussia and was once known as The White Horse and King of Prussia, much to the distress of drunks. The old hotel, billiard room and stables for 40 horses were rebuilt in the 1940s. Today the pub caters for families on outings and they obviously agree with the Prince Regent's view of Rottingdean as "' a pleasant and delightful village, with a good inn." THE BLACK HORSE, no relation to the white one, is an inn in the High Street and THE PLOUGH, also modernised, stands within sight and sound of the duck pond by the village green. Sometimes the noise inside The Plough, on a busy day, makes the mallards take flight before somebody decides that they would make an excellent roast lunch.

Rottingdean is close to Brighton on the main road leading from Kemp Town. In Brighton there are over 200 pubs from which to choose but two in The Lanes, THE BATH ARMS (Union Street) and THE DRUID'S HEAD (Brighton Place) have managed to retain a period flavour in their contents which is more than can be said for the beer you buy today. THE GOLDEN FLEECE is also in The Lanes area and so is THE CRICKETERS HOTEL, once a coaching inn that was known as The Laste and Fishcart in the 18th century. The pub is next door to the site of the Old Black Lion Brewery, now demolished, which was functioning when fish was measured by the laste. THE GREYHOUND, with a history of smuggling linked with Pool Valley, is in East Street within sound of the sea. You can glimpse the sea from THE PUMP HOUSE, Market Street, a Regency-style pine panelled pub restored in 1954. The building stands on land which may have formed part of the Cluniac Monastery of Bartholomews before destruction by fire during a French raid in 1514. The position of this pub is ideal for weary shoppers and so is THE SUSSEX, within crawling distance of the taxi-rank if your legs collapse. THE DOWNS

HOTEL, at Woodingdean, is between Brighton and Rottingdean if your taxi is travelling in either direction. This is a mid-1920s pub that stands on a windy summit with views of sea, sky and streets of houses, billowing like ribbons over the landscape. The atmosphere of the pub is jovial with the boisterous spirits that one associates with labradors and spaniels.

Juggs were men who used to transport fish from Brighton to Lewes in baskets on their backs. The JUGGS ARMS is a cottage-style pub enhanced by an orchard at Kingston, just outside Lewes. You would expect a cider with Rosie in the comfortable interior, where the ingle-nook is several centuries old and where the Juggs raised their jars in another age. In nearby Lewes there are several fine drinking places in the High Street. THE PELHAM ARMS has a 15th century heritage, cheerful log fires in winter and excellent food all the year. THE SHELLEYS HOTEL, lower down the hill, is architecturally and historically interesting. The original building was dated 1577 and in the 17th century was sold to the Shelley family by the Earl of Dorset. Enlargements were made in the 18th century to meet the needs of travellers in coaches. The interior is too opulent to qualify as an ordinary pub, but comfort is the keynote and one is reminded of the times when there was less haste and less speed. THE WHITE HART is also an hotel in the High Street and, like Shelleys, has fine furniture and paintings preserved from earlier centuries when it belonged to the Parker and Pelham families. Today, squires and lawyers, from the County Court, mix silk with tweeds and pipe-sucking swains mix with pale, well-spoken girls sipping sherry.

Those who prefer the tang of the sea to the call of the countryside will be more at home in the pubs at Pagham, Shoreham, Southwick, Hastings, Rye and Winchelsea. The variety of scenery should cater for all tastes but the atmosphere is equally salty in each of the coastal towns. THE LAMB INN is 16th century, beamed and braced for those who reach it when they travel between Bognor and Chichester. The pub is at Nyetimber, part of Pagham, where there are sea breezes, a seabird sanctuary and a Pram Race on Boxing Day for landlubbers. THE SCHOONER, at Southwick on the coast, overlooks Shoreham Harbour. People who use the pub look nautical; some own the boats moored in the lock and speak knowledgeably on seafaring matters. Some customers wear nautical clothes but their only experience of the sea seems to be a drunken totter to starboard at closing time. Shoreham-By-Sea is linked to Southwick by the main road and on it THE CROWN AND ANCHOR is landmarked by a ship's figurehead, a sailor rocking his boat, outside. The atmosphere is so appropriate for the area that you may be tempted to burst into a sea shanty after a session in the pub. THE RED LION, by the Toll Bridge over the River Adur in Shoreham, has 16th century history but the decorations and prints are a legacy from the times when stage coaches made the pub a stopping point.

The fishermen's tall wooden huts at Hastings were used for hanging and drying the nets and today make an unusual contribution to seaside ephemera. THE ROYAL STANDARD, in Bourne Street, has been used by fishermen since the 19th century. Hastings is one of the Cinque Ports and the house which commemorates King Harold's last stand by its name is near that fatal hill at Senlac. In the Royal Standard you can once again imagine that you are drinking in a fishing village untroubled by tourist traffic, which is left outside or parked on the Fishmarket.

On the borders of Kent, in an area of flat marshland there is another of the Cinque Ports, Rye, which stands on a hill, marooned when the sea receded. It seems miraculous that this fine town is still standing after a harsh history and the violence that came when raids were made from the French coast in the 14th century. THE KING'S HEAD, is a peaceful pub today, with parts that have survived for two hundred years. THE MERMAID, in cobbled and clap-boarded Mermaid Street, epitomises what tourists expect an English pub to look like. Whole trees form the cross beams inside, the fireplace is large enough to roast and serve an oxen and the windows, as well as the floors, slope before you've had a drink. There are also rooms for overnight visitors, who will appreciate the authentic period trimmings. THE PIPEMAKER'S ARMS also has authentic trimmings which include oak beams and a quaint collection of pipes for study by smokers, not plumbers. Winchelsea, another of the Cinque Ports, has had a similar record of raids by the French, and ravages from the sea a century earlier, like Rye. The Strand Gate stands on a hill above the marshland like a lonely landmark. YE OLDE CASTLE INN also stands ruggedly defiant and dates back to the 14th century, with smugglers cellars that are no longer used. There are modern touches in the interior, warmth and comfort. The pub is as solid and dependable as Tom Sayers, the prizefighter, who fought sixty rounds without gloves in the garden in 1850.

The names of Sussex pubs are frequently linked with their history but how do you explain THE SHOULDER OF MUTTON AND CUCUMBER'S name at Yapton, a village on the road to Bognor? Apparently this was a Sussex dish set before travellers after long coach journeys in the 18th century. The pub is as plain, externally, as the dish it is named after but there is a warm welcome for visitors when they step inside. THE GALLIPOT, at Hartfield, has an unusual name derived from the small pots of ointment that were brought from the Mediterranean in galleys. But the place is a splendid example of the charm to be found in Sussex pubs. The Gallipot is a Tudor-style cottage, mellow and hospitable, with tiled floors, horse brasses and open fires. What more could you ask for when you're thirsty and tired?

Not every pub in Sussex is visually attractive, but the majority have an air of permanence which sometimes has greater appeal for their users than beauty. Fortunately, however, the memory of pleasing buildings is less liable to destruction than those buildings we have come to regard as permanent. They can suddenly disappear, in the wake of new planning, almost as quickly as a pint of beer does.

The Terminal Building and Roof Office Block at Gatwick Airport
Architects: Yorke Rosenberg Mardall

Brighton Station
constructed in 1840 and still bustling with life
(Reproduced by courtesy of the Evening Argus.)

Ex Great Western Railway 4-4-0
3217 Earl of Berkeley nears Freshfield with the 3.55 p.m. from
Sheffield Park to Horsted Keynes

Shoreham Harbour
with Brighton and piers in the background

16. Brighton's Lanes.
Straight and Narrow Paths

The openings, for speaking through the glass fronts to counters of modern banks and Post Offices, are decreasing in size. Soon they will be too narrow to push a banana through. There are no banks in The Lanes at Brighton and the nearest Post Office is in Ship Street, where you can enter one lane, Union Street. The other entrances are off North Street, where the banks bunch together in mutual confidence, Prince Albert Street, at the side of Lane End House, and Market Street. The entrances are indicated by badly designed signposts, which can easily be missed if your height is normal, and there is an absence of litter bins. This fact encourages those who eat in the streets to act like pigs in paper clover.

Brighton's Lanes, the adjoining streets and the church of St. Nicholas are the architectural remnants of the old fishing village called Brighthelmstone. The village was sacked by French raiders in 1514 and they only left the church intact. Fishermen's cottages were all that made up the central area of the town before 1700. The area had been well-trodden by Neolithic man and The Lanes, in the 17th century, were merely pathways used to delineate gardens and plots of land. The Meeting House was one of the earliest buildings, built in 1698, when Meeting House linked with Black Lion Street and it's still there today.

In the 19th century, houses of earlier periods in the area were rebuilt and the original pattern of the pathways began to change. Some old flint and pebble walls may have remained from medieval times but The Lanes were built up in the 18th century and the early part of the 19th century. The first shop to open was a fishmonger's, prepared to trade in the midst of fishermen's houses. The shores of Sussex were surrounded by fish then, as they are now. But today we are offered fish-fingers, effete cuts, which are a dainty substitute for cod steaks and whole haddocks. The fishmonger, the coal merchant and the milkman, known as the cow keeper, were the first traders to begin business in The Lanes. The milkman's fresh milk was doubtful because the cows were kept in backyard byres, unhygienic places that could curdle blood, let alone milk. Shops and workrooms began to increase as Londoners, and people from other cities, came lemming-like to the seaside. The demand for shoemakers was immediate. Feet, in the Regency period, were a talking point rather than a walking point and a great deal of time was spent squeezing gouty, swollen limbs into small, hand-made slippers. And so Thomas Dekker's "brave shoemakers, all gentlemen of the gentle craft," stitched on to create new fashions, repair holes in dancing pumps and resole military boots.

Cabinet-makers were needed to provide furniture for the new houses that Kemp was building at Kemp Town, as well as for the new houses in terraces and squares that were built for the enlarging population of Brighton. Bakers and beer shops, the first off-licences, flourished like the inns. The Laste and Fish Cart, now The Cricketers, The New Inn, now The Clarence Hotel, The Old Ship and The Druid's Head, in The Lanes, had no cause for complaint. Smugglers were kept busy in the tunnels that ran through the old cellars while drinking was the soldier's pleasure above them. The inns were usually full and nobody considered the idea of drinking whilst standing up barbaric because there wasn't room to fall down. In the heyday of the horse, later than the middle of the 17th century when coaches began carrying passengers on the five routes from London to the coast, coachmen, ostlers and postillions used the inns in The Lanes to slake their thirsts. The Four Aces Restaurant, in Poplar Place, was once a tavern and The Knab — Brighton Place today — was a gathering place for horsepower, when horses had it, where the hoarse shouts were as lusty as the ale brewed then.

The origins of The Lanes and subsequent buildings were humble but the fact that premises remaining today have been listed to avoid alterations that might be out of character, gives some indication of the architectural merit. The heart of the old town has been preserved and although The Lanes have been described as " Brighton's Kasbah ", or compared to the bazaars of North Africa, they are an English institution, a sheltered shopping area where you can window-gaze without risk. Vehicles can only be parked on the perimeter, where parking areas are totally inadequate for the volume of traffic. A parking space has become as valuable as a stick of jade, or an hour of time. The attraction of The Lanes is a powerful aphrodisiac for visitors. The individual parts are not endeavouring to vie against and outdo each other. They are an excellent example of the unity that can be achieved in architecture, a functional art, and express a harmony of social order grouped round a symbol of community unity, the Elim Church. This was the earliest non-conformist church in Brighton, the Union Chapel, which was built in 1683 although only one wall of cobble and red brick still exists. The church was rebuilt in 1825 by Amon Wilds, who designed the Grecian-style doorway which leads you into semi-circular shaped interior where there are cast iron columns with foliated capitals. The building is now occupied by the Elim Four Square Gospel Tabernacle, cheerful people with strong voices.

The Lanes suffered a decline when the size of the town increased, bringing in its wake bigger shops which were aimed to attract the early Victorian shoppers. New and bigger houses were also built to meet the new demands. Small shops began to decay in appearance and in terms of business, since the new population preferred wide thoroughfares or promenades on the seafront to the narrow alleys of The Lanes. You can under-stand the Victorian attitude of expecting high moral tone, cleanliness and value for their money when prosperity and a bright industrial future lay ahead of them. They preferred the style of instant Pugin to fishermen's revival. The Victorian habit of collecting curios and souvenirs was as dedicated as their enthusiasm for antiques of the 18th century, which were plentiful when the chattels of houses were sold at the declining Spas and found their way to Brighton, or Tunbridge Wells, for collectors to buy.

Eventually The Lanes deteriorated into slums, of which parts disappeared altogether as the 19th century ended and the 20th century began. In 1926, George Aitchison wrote: " The Lanes are one of the things of which Brighton does not speak. The Lanes are the poor old grandparents, whom the nouveau riche descendants find it convenient to ignore." But prosperity came again when Queen Mary, a connoisseur of antiques, found a great deal to her liking among the treasures she discovered while walking regally through The Lanes in the 1930s. Her visits, during her reign with George V, were events which stimulated business and attracted others to follow the lead set by royalty. Genuine antiques have never been cheap to buy. Some collectors acquire antiques by private purchase at prices which make dealers in The Lanes slightly angry. This jealousy is understandable when antiques, in fine condition, are a much sought after commodity. If the advice of dealers is good you can learn from it; if it isn't, you can dismiss it. But the mixed marriage of shops is not all bed and bric-a-brac. Some are so small that any wild gesture would endanger the objets d'art, objets trouvé and objets perdu. The dim interiors have concealed a multitude of fakes, furniture with horizontal wormholes and Continental copies of porcelain passing for Spode, Rockingham, Chelsea and Bow. The only genuine Bow, in many antique shops, was the window.

The Lanes, however, prospered from the revival of interest which patronage, that was part accolade and part royal aid, had bestowed on the area. When Queen Mary died, a large number of her acquisitions, which filled rooms in Buckingham Palace, found their way into the London auction rooms. Some of the antiques returned to Brighton and were offered for sale at prices far greater than anybody could have imagined before World War II. The Lanes today are no longer an exclusive area for antique buyers, who know that they are unlikely to find bargains. But tourists, residents and students are attracted to the narrow alleyways and the new style of shops, in which modern window dressing has replaced calculated disorder. The variety of shops has increased since the 'sixties and now include boutiques, record dealers, art galleries, suede specialists, confectioners, carpet-sellers, booksellers, fruiterers, jewellers, silversmiths, cabinet-makers and shoeshops. English's Oyster Bar and Wheeler's, for fish dishes, Zetland's and Forfars, for bread and cakes, are old established. Old blood leaves The Lanes but new blood ensures a continuous flow to the heart.

Union Street is a unique mixture, being the only lane with a church, a Chinese restaurant, a public house, a coffee bar, two art galleries and shops where you can buy silver, gold, porcelain, glass and bygones. Elsewhere in the area there are coffee bars, restaurants and public houses for all tastes. The new style of The Lanes reflects the taste of the second half of the 20th century when bright lights, speed and vitality have been the manifestations of the changes that occurred in our lives since the 'sixties. The currency of living has been cheapened and values made false during the period, according to critics who have not moved with the spirit of their times. But those shops whose goods have the benefit of being cheap also have the disadvantage of looking it. When new development was mooted for the old Lanes it produced a mild form of hysteria and indignation but when the scheme — Brighton Square — had been completed any fears that the new buildings, which were three storeys high only, would fail to express the spirit of the surroundings, were dispelled.

Brighton Square has been described as " a town-planning triumph ", which filled in back-land and received a Civic Trust Award in 1967. The development included 24 shops, 11 of which were grouped round the main square and the remainder led off from the corners of the square. Eleven maisonettes and four flats were built at first floor level, overlooking the square on three sides. A restaurant, pyramid roofed, made up the fourth side with a high-level terrace. A basement car park for 50 cars, was built under the square accessible by ramp. The architects for the development were Fitzroy Robinson and Partners, who used traditional finishes — tilehanging, shiplap boarding and flint-faced precast concrete panels — without diluting the impact of their modern buildings. The architecture related to the surroundings because of its intimate scale and because the sense of continuity, as well as enclosure, maintained the spirit of the surrounding alleys. On a fine day, the square attracts crowds and is actually used for sitting out as well as shopping. You don't hear nightingales singing in it but you do hear songs of praise.

The Lanes are a narrow maze of rebuilt properties that have not been shattered by the misplaced discords of any architectural style. At night they are a silent picture and the talking version of it by day.

17. Marine Palace. King of the Pagodas

The Regency age was flamboyant and produced the Royal Pavilion, Brighton's famous landmark, a bizarre architectural fantasy that has to be seen to be disbelieved. The building is picturesque and functional but expresses the paradoxes of the period which is linked, inseparably, with the Prince Regent. He visited Brighton in 1783 on the advice of his physicians and to escape from the moods of his over-strict father. He married Mrs. Fitzherbert in 1785 and rented Kemp's Farm from his steward. The site was on the West side of the Steine, where the Royal Pavilion was to be built.

Brighton was growing into a fashionable resort towards the close of the 18th century, attracting social butterflies and rakes like Richard Barry, seventh Earl of Barrymore, who tramped the streets of Brighton with his two brothers and Tom Hooper, their hired prize-fighter, following behind dressed as a clergyman. He used his fists when the brothers chose to pick a fight with someone. Six streets existed in Brighton at that time, East and West Street, Middle and North Street, with Black Lion Street and Ship Street, both named after taverns. The remainder of the fishing village consisted of brick and timber cottages, faced with tarred weatherboarding or knapped flints, and the church of St. Nicholas. The Lanes, too, were old Brighton when the village was called Brighthelmstone and faithless wives put their hands over the reflections in looking-glasses as though to keep secrets.

John Nash was a secretive man and was the architect who transformed Henry Holland's classical villa for the prince into a Royal Palace, beginning his commission in 1815. He supplanted Repton, the originator of the Oriental extravaganza, in the Prince Regent's favour and ingratiated himself with the Carlton House coterie. Repton, fortunately, had other projects to keep him well occupied including improvements to the stately home of Uppark and its grounds in Sussex. Nash's relationships with other architects were unrealistic and, because of his social success, he aroused jealousy and criticism of his work among other professionals. He met a better type of enemy in the social circles he moved through until eventually even placid Sir John Soane was goaded to fury after Nash took over the drawings, prepared by Soane, of Buckingham Palace. On that occasion, the architect of the Royal Pavilion excelled himself with a display of teasing, histrionics and facetiousness which would have made a saint swear.

Kemp's Farm was rebuilt by Henry Holland, the architect who was given a free hand as consolation for giving up work on Carlton House. He completed a cream painted, symmetrical villa on the site in 1787 after five months' work. The plan had a central circular drawing room with semi-circular apses, communicating on each side with pairs of additional reception rooms. The building was the nucleus of the Pavilion as it exists today. The shallow bay windows and domed Ionic peristyle were in the manner of a country house. The green painted tent-shaped canopies were added over the balconies between the years 1801 to 1804. During this period the interior decoration was Chinese in style.

Nash began his improvements in 1815, building without Treasury sanction and embodying over thirty years thought. He had been appointed Deputy Surveyor General and Controller of the Board of Works when James Wyatt, the favourite of George the Third, was killed in his carriage in 1813. Smirke and Soane, prospective candidates for the appointment, had fresh fire for their hatred of Nash but were appointed as architects for a separate part of public development under the office of works. Nash started on the Royal Pavilion by adding two large rooms to the existing villa, which lacked a music room and a banqueting room. The original reception rooms had already been enlarged. The west front was extended to include two entrance vestibules, the royal bedroom, the library and guest rooms with a long gallery. The kitchen and servants' quarters, always noisy places and a hotbed of gossip, were attached to the south wing which was concealed by shrubbery.

The late works of many important artists and architects tend towards self-parody. Nash escaped this fate since there was a fashionable Indian cult at the time and the scents of the East wafted on the breeze in Brighton. Tented domes and minarets expressed the new rooms externally. The original bow fronts were capped with onion domes and finials while the centre dome, larger than the rest, was built over the original drawing room. The result has inspired wits to make waspish comments in two centuries and at the time when the antique statues, frozen in gestures of reproof, were removed from the original gardens. The green trellised balconies, which looked towards the sea, were also removed by Nash and replaced by arched verandahs of pierced stone, suitably crenellated, intended to unify the main elements. The elaborate external detail and the carefully considered silhouette were eventually the main assets of the composition.

Roger Fulford, describing the Pavilion, has written: " As with most Regency houses, the bedrooms were sacrificed to the living rooms." Nash kept to his schedule with the Prince Regent at one end and the Pavilion at the other. He was not the type of man to waste time plucking forbidden fruit or being side-tracked from his ambition. The internal decorations of the marine palace were extravagent and in the colours and designs of fashionable Chinoisserie. Pink and Chinese blue were chosen, with motifs of bamboo, leaves and birds. The banqueting room alone was a pâstiche, combining classical coves and spandrels, multi-coloured decorations and a weird ceiling. The ceiling was painted with plantain leaves, supplemented by additional free standing leaves which surrounded a silver and green dragon. The dragon's mouth spouted forth a litter of smaller dragons, gilded birds and lotus blossoms that surrounded the central crystal chandelier. You wouldn't have called it dignified, but it was certainly breath-taking. The windows were lozenge shaped, framed with crimson silk which completed the scheme of decoration. The total effect was excessive and beyond analysis but it contained the necessary magnificence to satisfy the royal client, who saw in it a reflection of his own adventures.

The subsidiary rooms, restrained in decoration and with the original ceiling heights unaltered, made a pleasant relief for visitors. Even these rooms, however, were redecorated on numerous occasions before Nash was satisfied with the results. The music room, complete with organ, wall paintings of Chinese origin, orange and gold decorations, blue carpet and curtains, contained another chandelier which was shaped like a water lily. This was supplemented by eight smaller ones, literally gilding the lily. The domed ceiling was decorated with gold scallop shells which diminished in the tradition of coffering. The Royal Marines have a dance band, which played in the music room during the Commemoration Ball held to mark the 150th anniversary of the coronation of George the Fourth in June 1971. The accoustics were so good that the notes from the brass instruments rattled the moondrops on the chandeliers as the band played on. The scallop shells and shell-like ears withstood the test of trumpeting.

Elegance was not Nash's intention, and his determination to create an unrivalled oriental fantasy was greatly assisted by the furniture designs of Robert Jones, who imported some of the pieces from China. But it may have been Nash's wife, Mary Ann Bradley, who made the greatest contribution. Mary, daughter of a coal merchant, had married Nash in 1798 at St. George's, Hanover Square, when she was twenty five and he was forty six. Between 1815 and 1823 (when the Pavilion was completed) Mary, according to public ballads, broadsheets and innuendo, had been mistress of the Prince Regent. The questions, unanswered, are whether Nash married her because he was aware of her strength in the royal bed or whether she became a royal favourite subsequently. Nash was not a rich man at the time of his marriage. Few architects of the period, however successful they were, could have afforded his mansion in Dover Street and the estate on the Isle of Wight. He appeared to live beyond his means and his marriage, on the surface, appears to have been one of convenience. Mary, it seems, made her contribution to Nash's public success not by standing up for him but by lying down.

Many people, like Queen Victoria, were not amused by George IV's oriental caprice. The young queen, after the first shock of visiting Brighton had worn off, decided that the exotic building was unsuitable as a royal residence. " A strange, odd Chinese looking thing," she commented, " and from it you could only see a little morsel of the sea." She therefore removed the best furniture in 1847 and left the building empty until it was purchased by the Town Commissioners in 1850 for £53,000, which was a bargain considering that the final cost of the building had been £500,000. The rooms were stripped of their decorations and fittings, leaving only the ceilings intact. But the dark paintwork, which replaced the finery as a sop to Victorian morality, failed to destroy the spirit of the Pavilion and its history of amorous escapades.

The Pavilion was intended to provide an escape from the restrictions of life. The Prince was made Regent in 1811 when he was the recognised leader of high society. His legs had thickened and the late hours, drinking bouts and pursuit of women had coarsened his features. Tantrums were frequent as his temper frayed and friendship with him become hazardous, like the corset he wore to disguise his swollen figure. The family background, Hanoverian, expressed itself in vulgarity, madness and stupidity but, despite this heritage, the Prince developed a passionate taste for beauty and aesthetic feelings to justify the description " the First Gentleman in Europe." He loved horses with almost as much passion as he loved women and his sporting friends included Sir John Lade, Sir John Shelley, the Duke of Bedford and the Earl of Jersey. Gambling and women, however, revealed the Prince's capacity for spending and were manias with him.

Most women prefer to be looked over rather than be overlooked, even in our present era of emancipation and sexual freedom. Heroes today may no longer swashbuckle, swing from trees and gallop to the rescue but they are expected to be red-blooded and not suffer from pernicious anaemia. The unique, nostalgic smells of sea and stables can evoke, for me, a sense of the Regency scene. But the Prince Regent as an ardent lover is harder to imagine, despite records of the charm, intelligence and vivacity which endeared him to his friends. The pictures left by historians and portrait painters seldom reveal these qualities and the attributes that made him attractive to a wide circle of women of different backgrounds. His generosity with gifts of money or land, for favours received, was an obvious attraction as well as the prestige for a lady of being hand-picked, and probably hand-pinched, by royalty.

After the battles that had raged at sea, Copenhagen and Trafalgar, the land-owners, the rich farmers and the wartime contractors — for clothing — were prosperous. Wealth and display, glitter and sport were expressions of the beau monde and aristocratic families who had inherited the accumulated wealth of the 18th century. Money was squandered in the pursuit of pleasure despite the appalling conditions of the poor and the general mood of unrest due to unemployment. Rioting and machine-breaking were commonplace when machines began to destroy the village crafts. The frustrated poor gave vent to their emotions by violence. You can see a parallel in the strikes and tensions of the present century but in Regency times patronage was plentiful and nobody laid down rules or pointed the direction for morals and creative work. Even the Pavilion, all pumpkins and pepper boxes, was not considered to be an extravagance.

Prinny, whatever his looks may have suggested, was seldom at a loss for words. Loss of breath was another matter. His gluttony for game pie was known to overcome him even during the pursuit of a desirable woman. Beau Brummell, who caught the eye of both sexes, discovered the Regent as he paused to consume a chunk of flaky pastry in the midst of a chase with a serving girl. "I hope that I am never that damned hungry," remarked Brummell. "You will be," retorted the Prince, still eating, "but that may be afterwards." Fortunately, in those days, a paunch was considered to be a sign of good breeding, as were aristocratic ankles. Many aristocratic feet can be heard, on a still summer day, tapping a ghostly staccato within the walls of the Pavilion but who were the women, from fish-seller to Duchess, who pleasured Prinny when the whim took him?

Anyone who was able to please him and amuse him, as Beau Brummell did, was eligible. No tender ballad called women to the man who was the foremost libertine of an extremely promiscuous age. The Prince was witty, though tender hearted, and showed considerable understanding of Mrs. Fitzherbert's nature throughout their times together. She could be extremely off-hand with him when the mood of jealousy overcame her normally generous nature. In July, 1821, Maria Fitzherbert had the satisfaction of knowing that Queen Caroline was locked out of Westminster Abbey and forced to drive away from the Coronation of King George the Fourth while she remained his uncrowned queen. She had, however, to ignore her husband's taste for the " Fashionable Impures ", the demi-mondaines, who had at their head Harriette Wilson, a famous and witty courtesan of the Regency period.

When Harriette Wilson was 15, with a mane of thick, dark hair cascading over her shoulders. she galloped her favourite mare in the Steine. Inevitably, the Prince Regent sent for her, by messenger, to come to town and " have an interview." Miss Wilson promptly replied to the invitation with her usual self-assurance: " To travel 52 miles this bad weather, merely to see a man, with only the given number of legs, arms, fingers, etcetera, would, you must admit, be madness in a girl like myself, surrounded by humble admirers who are ever ready to travel any distance for the honour of kissing the tip of her little finger." Modesty was not her strong suit and it is not surprising that, when she published her memoirs in 1825 in paper cover parts, so great was the demand that a barrier had to be erected in the publisher's shop to regulate the crowd of buyers. The memoirs had been written with blackmail in view and those who refused to pay to have their adventures erased from Harriette Wilson's passionate narrative were described regardless of whether their parts, in her life, were large or small.

Butterflies, when pinned down, are entitled to a final desperate flutter of their wings. Lady Jersey had the summer charm and delicacy of a butterfly when she was a grandmother, aged 40, in 1794. That handsome and attractive woman snared the Prince by letting him believe he had hunted and succeeded in pinning her down. Her influence over him was sufficiently strong to make him write to Mrs. Fitzherbert and state that he would never enter her house again. Mrs. Fitzherbert prompty left her Brighton house, with dignity and a scathing description of Lady Jersey's main asset, and proceeded to travel abroad discreetly for a few months. During the period of his attachment to Lady Jersey, the Prince had debts of more than half a million pounds, due mainly to his habit of scattering annuities and gifts of money to those who pleased him. Mrs. Crouch, a dubious lady, held his bond for £10,000 but would have much preferred a little ready cash.

The Regent's debts were not all attributable to gambling and many were incurred through the adventurers of both sexes with whom he surrounded himself. Mrs. Fitzherbert was not greedy, but even she had an allowance of £10,000 a year and frequent gifts of jewellery to appease her outbursts of temper. And when the Prince married Princess Caroline of Brunswick, as a means of paying off his debts, Lady Jersey became — appropriately — Lady of the Bedchamber. She put Epsom salts in the Princess's supper on the wedding night to remind the Prince of her presence in his household. Mrs. Fitzherbert may have meant more to Prinny than any of his passing fancies but this didn't stop his association with Lady Jersey or prevent him drinking from her glass in public. He even gave her his wife's pearl bracelets as a gift when she admired them hoping that this would happen. Lady Jersey retained her hold until 1796 when her reign came to its end. The Duchess of Devonshire and Lady Jerningham (a staunch Catholic) were old friends of the Prince and were well satisfied to see a schemer go.

Mrs. Fitzherbert resumed her old life with Prinny in 1799, having received an assurance from the Pope that there were no obstacles in the way of reconciliation, except for the proviso that he should be repentant and ready to make amends. They were both, at that time, poor but happy which was an admirable state of affairs for true lovers but not so satisfactory for their creditors. The fact that Prinny had no money in his royal pocket made no difference to his extravagancies. When the Prince was pleasantly tipsy, which was most of the time despite Mrs. Fitzherbert's efforts to keep him sober, he made sure that he was surrounded by rowdy company. " How many wives have you had?" the Regent was asked by a companion of the Duke of Greevey. " You mean apart from my own?" he was reputed to have replied, not so intoxicated as to forget the respect that Mrs. Fitzherbert demanded. He never worried about a wasp chasing him when there was a lion lurking in the undergrowth.

Lady Barrymore and her sister, the Duchess de Castries, both Irish peasant girls, were newcomers to the royal circle but were welcomed as favoured guests to the Pavilion in 1804. They were amusing story-tellers, gifted with the Irish sense of the dramatic, and were able to give first-hand accounts of their childhood when they had helped their parents to sell locally-distilled whiskey to smugglers. Lady Clermont was another good spinner of yarns. She was one of Prinny's favourites and enjoyed a nip of brandy, secret or otherwise. Fortified, Lady Clermont graced the Pavilion with her aureole of orange light and spoke swiftly with a great deal of misguided enthusiasm. She excused her hiccups and unsteady gait as being the result of old age, too many adventures and a naturally irritable nature. To Lady Clermont might be attributed the Mallapropism, if not the original character, of: "One swallow doesn't make a slummer."

Lady Nagle, another Irishwoman, claimed that she had two hearts of gold since she always wore a miniature of her husband in a locket on her breast. Her husband, Commander of the Brighton Sea Fencibles, was the butt of her practical jokes, even accepting a gift of his own horse, coated with whitewash, believing it to be a generous gesture by the Regent. Lady Haggerstone, Mrs. Fitzherbert's sister, who sometimes rented a house in Brighton for the season, was a dizzy lady who amused the Prince, particularly when she attempted to milk a bull at a fête champêtre in her garden. A young gallant, who was dressed in the flamboyant attire of the Hussars, praised her youthful appearance despite the disaster. He was told before she retired in confusion: "I am old enough to be your mother."

"Only if she was foolish enough to let herself be raped at 13," the Prince remarked when he was a tactful distance from Lady Haggerstone.

Apart from the succession of rowdy visitors to the Pavilion, life was fairly simple and enlivened by evening parties with plenty to drink. Dinner was served at six, and the women were limited to two — Mrs. Fitzherbert and one other — usually Lady Clermont, Lady Berkley or the Dowager Lady Sefton. It was not the custom, at that period, to have equal numbers of each sex at table. Whist, a card game which Mrs. Fitzherbert enjoyed, invariably followed the meal. At 10 o'clock a new batch of guests arrived, including a suitable selection of women and the evening settled into an amiable pattern of drinking, gossiping and musical entertainment. Prinny contributed his share of glee singing, sadly lacking a sense of rhythm, and occasionally played the cello, either alone, or in duets with Captain Bloomfield. Anyone who could perform was expected to do so and, of the performance that occurred after the music-making and drinking, the less said the better. Port has a great deal to be said in its favour, despite any twinges of gout or conscience that it may provoke. Sometimes the Prince and

Mrs. Fitzherbert dined out, taking with them their intimate friends as well as his entourage. High spirits usually abounded and the Prince was recorded as being " in great affability and Good Humour, making jokes and laughing most heartily " when he visited Lady Jerningham's house.

Today, the Royal Pavilion stands restored. The restoration reflected the care and knowledge of Clifford Musgrave, art historian and retired Director of the Royal Pavilion, who understood the single mindedness and ambition that had created one of the most spectacular regal follies in Europe. It was built in the Age of Elegance, an age when dandies strolled to their clubs and smart phaetons, with yellow wheels, went at a spanking pace along the Brighton road. Military uniforms enlivened the street scene and men like Beau Brummell shocked, intrigued and set the lead for elegant dressing. In furniture and architecture a strange mixture existed, a mixture of refinement, clumsiness, pretentiousness and, in some cases, the wildly bizarre. The pursuit of love was coupled with a taste for lively company. Pursuits that, even today, are as tempting as a siren song. But sirens, in mythology, are ladies of splendid promise and disappointing performance, unlike those who graced the Royal Pavilion.

18. Travel in Sussex.
Harbours, Hangars and Halts

In September, 1969, the Architectural Review pinpointed the spread of sailing, and the situation which existed then, in these words: "The sport of the rich man and the not so rich is played out against a shortage of moorings. Once at sea, the lonely sailor turns his back on the invasion of the beaches."

The coastal towns of Sussex are already overcrowded and for boating enthusiasts the lack of moorings is acute at resorts within reach of large cities. This has created a demand for planned harbours to serve yachts and small boats. Life afloat is also one solution for those who enjoy the sea and who cannot find, or build, suitable houses within reach of London and other cities. Suitable sites for parking boats in Sussex have to answer the problems of amenities, topography and acceptable planning.

Shoreham is a harbour port that caters for all types of boats and was established before the Norman conquest when Aelle, a Saxon chieftain, made his invasion from the sea before the Kingdom of the South Saxons was founded in A.D. 477. When Edward III invaded France in 1346, 26 of his ships came from Old Shoreham, where man-o-wars were built. King John claimed his crown at Shoreham when he landed after the death of Richard I and Charles II escaped from the port after his defeat at Worcester in 1651. Timber ships were built and sailed from the harbour until the 19th century when iron vessels began to replace them. Shoreham's heyday, as a port of embarkation for the Continent, has passed like the ship-building activities but the town has the opportunity of future prosperity. This could be achieved by increasing the area for houseboats to anchor between sea and land. Proposals for The Saltings roused public wrath but static moorings would provide accommodation, which is badly needed, for visiting sailors on their Friday to Monday boat-rocking jaunts even if this entails hammocks for the homesick. Merchantmen, who also dock at Shoreham, are increasing and already provide a Common Market link between Sussex and Europe.

Marinas have been designed to enable boat owners to board their vessels during any tide without leaving land. They originated in the United States in the late 'twenties of this century and were artificially created harbours which could provide large numbers of waterfront moorings. The existing natural harbours in Sussex lie in sheltered places surrounded by buildings that are functional, crisp in outline and built of sturdy materials that can withstand bad weather. The harbours give direct access to towns from the seaside, where housing has a diversity of character. Compare the spacious accommodation planned and built by Thomas Read Kemp on his estate at Kemp Town, Brighton, in 1827 and the fishermen's cottages at Rye, which are delightfully snug but not always sanitary.

New artificial harbours for Sussex were established in the mid 'sixties. Chichester Harbour is fortunate in having 27 square miles of water for the passage of ships and yacht centres have been built on the navigable inlets. Chichester Yacht Basin in Birdham was planned for the increasing number of berths that would be required by the 'seventies and was a far-sighted venture like the Cresta Marine at Newhaven, where there are all services and a private radio station. Newhaven is an important commercial centre and the yachting centre with marina is a natural progression. Yachts also race from Bishopstone and Seaford. Boats can be hired from sailing clubs in Bexhill, Eastbourne, Hastings and Pevensey Bay as well as Bosham Sea School, where there are summer regattas. All types of boats can be hired at Brooklands Pleasure Park at Worthing, a town where the ozone, a condensed form of oxygen with a refreshing odour, seems to have revived the retired and brought on a nautical fever.

Clubs and sailing clubs at Littlehampton, Felpham, Bognor Regis, Pagham Beach and Worthing, like numerous other clubs, have had two main problems to overcome — the provision of the maximum number of moorings possible and the necessary efficient service, with amenities, for those people who use them. These problems also dictate the siting of artificial harbours where a further consideration has been the surroundings. Static yachtsmen look inland rather than seaward. There are parts of Shoreham and Newhaven that need to be made ship-shape if the surroundings are to attract rather than repel. You can't anticipate the arrival of Morning Cloud when the setting you offer would be more suited to junks. Boats, unlike other forms of transport, can add beauty

The Seven Sisters Cliffs from Cuckmere Haven
The National Trust bought 632 acres of these cliffs and downs in 1940
(Reproduced by courtesy of The National Trust)

Lancing College, founded in 1848 by Nathaniel Woodward
The chapel, on the exposed site above the Adur, is a memorable piece of
architecture by R. C. Carpenter.

Photograph: Mike Jackson

St. George's Chapel at Kemp Town, Brighton
A typical Regency church built by C. A. Busby
for Kemp in 1825

Photograph: Richard Pike

Clapboard facing to one of the unique
buildings at Rye

to the soft, rural landscape with their shapely hulls and array of masts.

Marinas can be an initial success and then, like the first night triumph of an eccentric actress, decline through lack of capacity, like the play, as they continue to run. Centres for sailing along the Sussex coast are popular and France is accessible. Regattas, held at Bognor Regis, Hastings and Bexhill during the summer months attract a large number of entries. The Regatta in Brighton is a mid-June event with power-boat racing and rowing races. Those who steer in these events don't have time to rock the boat. The creation of a marina is costly for the developer, who has to overcome the difficulties of leasing the foreshore and finding an adequate depth of offshore water. The Brighton Marina Act was passed in 1968 and gave the developers the right to start work on the foreshore at Black Rock — leased to them for 125 years — for their £40 million harbour development.

The ambitious development for Brighton was revised several times until finally provision had been made for mooring 2,450 yachts, a yacht club with boat store and workshops. The Company responsible for the marina also planned for 1,000 flats and houses served by restaurants, public houses, shops and a sports centre. A conference centre and exhibition hall, plus parking for 6,000 cars, were also included to increase the value of the harbour to the town. Planning for the new requirements of yachtsmen using the coastline of the county will mean larger car parks and increased costs for the social amenities. The compensation, it has been suggested, will be better value for money although you may believe, as I do, that you can't have clean air with increased transportation and communication systems. Sussex has been a rich place to plunder when progress was the spearhead and money was the defence. Sussex-by-the-Sea could suffer, in the near future, from a new form of coastal erosion, resulting from marina-mania.

A century ago, when certain forms of development could still be as destructive to the landscape as they are today, man was not airborne. In the 19th century another Sussex, in the United States near Milwaukee, was "named for County Sussex, England, home of prominent pioneers. First settlers were George Elliott and Richard Cooling in 1843." One year later, in this country, 2,000 passengers started their journey from London Bridge at 8.30 in the morning on the first excursion train travelling through Sussex. They finally steamed under the Victorian canopies of Brighton Station just in time for a shrimp and whelk tea. The railway map of England in 1848 was "Bradshaw" and since the railways covered 5,000 miles of the country, after their approval by Queen Victoria, the idea of an annual holiday at the seaside spread among all classes. Reduced prices for family tickets and excursions encouraged trips, particularly when the cost of a Third Class return ticket from London to Brighton was only 3/6d. The trains of the mid 19th century were picturesque and noisy, puffing and steaming across the new tracks through Sussex until they reached a station. They are archaic today, when the hiss of coal power has been replaced by the pneumatic brakes of electric and diesel transport, but their charm remains like that of a dusty, childhood toy.

Oscar Wilde never travelled without his diary, explaining that one should always have something sensational to read in the train. Trains don't always run to time and when the railways were built across the county a new meaning was given to minutes. You may be one of those people who do not care about time but there are people who are idealistic and care about preserving bygones. Preservation doesn't always pay but one exception in Sussex is the Bluebell Railway at Sheffield Park, one of the steam railways that still survives. The branch line, preserved by enthusiasts, runs on 5 miles of track through pleasant countryside to Horsted Keynes. The line was closed by British Rail in 1958 and they wanted £55,000 for the land, stations, track and fittings between the two terminal stations. They finally accepted £34,000 and leased the booking office at Sheffield Park for a weekly rental of five shillings. Today, the track and rolling stock bought by the Bluebell Preservation Society is a profitable tourist attraction used by ½ million visitors a year.

The Bluebell Railway has a permanent full-time staff of five but a much larger number of enthusiastic, unpaid volunteers who help operate the line and look after the nine locomotives, which date back to 1870. The locomotives still have their original names and, I think, their own personalities when they answer to names which include Bluebell, Primrose and Stepney. There are 14 coaches, including the restored, brown ale coloured saloon of the London, Brighton and South Coast directors of 1914. The nostalgia for the steam age is supplemented by a practical policy of preserving trains which operated in the South of England and of selecting the best examples of engines. The servicing and repair work on the locomotives is carried out at Sheffield Park, where you'll find a station platform that is a splendid example of the use of Victorian cast iron columns which formed part of railway architecture. A collection of old advertisements are an amusing reminder of a robust age. When you travel along the track in the heart of Sussex, where the bluebells grow wild in early summer, you will enjoy a venture that is profitable and educational for those who have never seen, or heard, a steam engine.

Transport of the past is also preserved in Britain's first electric railway, which carries half a million passengers along Brighton's seafront, between the Palace Pier and Black Rock, each season. The inventor was Magnus Volk, who opened the railway in August, 1883, as an attraction for holidaymakers. The rolling stock may look quaint today, but it was conceived at a time when the first telephone and electric light systems were installed in Brighton at Volk's house on the Western Road. Magnus Volk was the son of a German clockmaker and, as a super sparks, supervised the electrical installation when it was used for the first time in the Royal Pavilion.

British Rail are often criticised, sometimes unfairly, for the service and standard of their trains. Improvements, however, are made each year as the outgoing and incoming tide of commuters, swollen by holidaymakers, increases. There are also a formidable number of tourists, students from overseas and lost, little old ladies, to control and understand. The telephone service at Brighton Station extends over a triangular area of Sussex, linking Eastbourne, Littlehampton and Balcombe. One of the most famous trains of this century was The Brighton Belle — formerly The Southern Belle — which started in the 'thirties as a string of restaurant cars. British Rail took over the running of the unique service for hungry travellers from the Pullman Company. The food was cooked in an area six feet by eight feet despite the lush trappings in which it was served and eaten. The regular theatrical passengers included Lord and Lady Olivier, Dame Flora Robson, Sir John and Lady Clements, Dora Bryan, Jimmie Edwards and Tommy Cooper. The final journey of The Brighton Belle was at the end of April, 1972, when the old lady bowed out in style, puffing a bit but game to the last. A chapter of railway history has been written to be celebrated, perhaps in the future, by an annual event.

On Madeira Drive, east of Brighton's Palace Pier, you can watch the Historical Commercial Vehicle Club Run, the Pioneer Club Run and the Race Cycle Tour of Great Britain as the vehicles spurt, sometimes with a touch of asthma in their engines, along the finishing stretch between March and May each year. The Veteran Car Run is held in November to mark the anniversary of the motorists first organised drive in 1896. Then they were celebrating the new Act which permitted road speeds of 14 miles an hour, except in places where local regulations reduced it to the alarming figure of 12 miles an hour. The

motorist, on that historic November day, had been emancipated
from the slavery of driving behind a man marching along the
road ahead waving a red flag. Cars like Genevieve, filmed and
famous, have chugged down the 54 miles of the Brighton Road
— usually with a breakdown in bad weather — where
previously 18th century coaches had thundered through the
towns of Reigate, Crawley and Handcross. Both forms of traffic
were spared the road jams that occur so frequently on the A.23
today. During the holiday season the road has become
notorious for its static line of sunlit ovens.

The increasing number of motorcars and other traffic passing
through Sussex necessitates new ideas in traffic management.
Motorists may eventually have to leave their vehicles at home,
or on the perimeter of towns, and use public transport. In
Sweden, the Tunnelbana subway — one of the best in Europe
— links Stockholm with the suburbs in less than half an hour.
Shopping areas are for pedestrians only and, despite the
standardisation of shops and street furniture, the elimination of
traffic hazards enables people to wander about without risk to
life and limb. In Sussex, where there is one vehicle for every
four people, the method of attracting drivers to use transport
other than their own will depend on the speed and ease of
travel offered by the alternatives. Bus-lanes only in certain
areas of the county would seem to be a sensible solution for
speeding up public transport and reducing road congestion.
New ideas have to be put into practice for public transport
unless we just sit back and wait until our towns are destroyed
by the increasing invasion of machines.

"Come fly with me," Frank Sinatra sang and he, too, may
have found flight preferable to being grounded by the problems
of motor growth. The London to Brighton road, and the
adjacent railway give simple and safe road or rail access to the
terminal building of Gatwick Airport. This major point of
entry, by aircraft, to the county is the first piece of architecture
that visitors from abroad see in Sussex. The design of the
buildings, by architects Yorke, Rosenberg and Mardall, is
impressive with admirable facilities for aircraft and passengers.
We tend to take good looking buildings for granted but when
the first stage of Gatwick Airport was completed in 1958 it was
well publicised and, later, praised by the public who were
pleased by the facilities. Gatwick, for Sussex, is a major
international airport at a time when air travel is still expanding. All types of air traffic are served and because this centre
now relieves Heathrow, the official London airport, visitors are
sometimes startled to find notices saying London (Gatwick)
Airport.

The airport has a fifty acre tarmac apron and the airfield lies beyond the runway. The car parks are generous in size but are overloaded and the road flyover takes you directly to the main entrance of the concourse. The main problem seems to be how to get rid of your car, if you drive yourself, which is a flaw in planning. The area of the airport could not be increased in size easily for future expansion due to the position of the runway road and the limit of the apron where the aircraft stand. The buildings, too, were not designed for an increase in height. The airport will have to accommodate future changes in aircraft design and social habits that will affect all types of transport in Sussex. The solution will depend on which way the hot air blows.

Changes in transport have also made themselves felt on farming in the county, where the functional wooden plough of the past was cheap even if you had to buy a family size pot of embrocation for your weary limbs. The ploughmen may have plodded but they had oxen to pull for them up to the end of the 19th century. The heavy soil of the Weald required beasts as strong and powerful as oxen, which were cheap to feed, yoke and groom. Oxen were also used to pull coaches up to the end of the 18th century when the mud of tracks and fields would have caused horses to flounder and fall. The horse, even the sepia coloured Sussex breed that had blonde manes and tails, were used for ploughing on the downland farms until mechanisation superseded them and added higher costs to a farmer's budget. Pope John said that there were three ways of losing money quickly — women, gambling and farming — and that farming was the dullest of all three. He was obviously wise enough to realise that only in heaven would the donkey, the early form of country transport, finally reach the elusive carrot which egged him on.

19. Tomorrow's Sussex. Symbols and Drums

The basilisk was a reptile which blasted by its breath or look, a lizard with crest inflated at will. Local Authorities, and those who dictate our future planning can be compared to that beast. So, too, can the developer who is prepared to destroy our heritage of buildings wilfully, and without authority, or defaces the landscape through lust for greater profit. New architecture in Sussex is too often pretentious and prone to gimmicks. Old architecture decays through neglect and lack of money for repairs. The surroundings in our rich and rewarding county are taken for granted by many of the inhabitants, who walk past buildings and landscape without realising they are there. When a view is obscured, or a building removed, they wake up and complain that they've been robbed.

Architecture changes, like the landscape, in varying lights and as you approach or recede from it. Inhuman new towns, where the roads give no relief for the eye, depress the spirit. Today's architects, sadly, stumble to find a solution for their shortcomings but use high sounding words for low key buildings. Words can enliven for us the things we should see, but they don't always succeed in their purpose. Lord Clark is a master of description and Sir John Betjeman is one of the most endearing recorders of architecture that has suffered from declining public interest. You meet some startling little fossils in the field of architecture and they give point to Winston Churchill's words: " We shape our buildings and, afterwards, our buildings shape us."

No building exists in a void. The surroundings and people should influence all architectural design but, despite this fact, the words of historians rarely convey any sense of setting by reference to town or country, landscape or climate. But the process of human development in the landscape of Sussex, and in the buildings after aesthetic consideration, is the concern of history if it is to have value in the future. The nature of Sussex is reflected in the materials of the buildings. The walls of houses are timber framed and tile-hung in the wooded clay area of the Weald. Cottages are faced with shiplap boarding in the forest areas where timber is plentiful and — by the sea — you'll find flint faced dwellings, some with flints knapped by hand, or Sussex cobbles trimmed at the corners of the houses by brick quoins. They have provided homes for farmworkers, foresters and fishermen who owe a debt to nature for their living.

The sea is as unpredictable as the sex of a seagull seen from a distance. But the misuse of the narrow belt of the coastline is predictable. The Scottish coastline, for climatic and other reasons, is relatively untouched but in Sussex the geography of the coast is changing swiftly. The value of the coast has made it subject to heavy pressures for development but the increasing demands made by marinas, seaside housing, transport centres and foreshore development have not yet wrecked the variety of scenery. There is one unhappy exception, Peacehaven, remnant of the First World War when it was named New Anzac by the Sea. The development provided the Englishman with his detached matchbox by the sea certainly, but the dwellings are sited cheek to jowl in hideous disorder and are a smear on the Sussex coastline.

The south coast is the most popular of all recreational areas but only about 50 miles of it are suitable for holiday resorts. Operation Neptune has preserved outstanding areas of natural beauty for future generations. In Sussex, vested interests have usually dominated public access to the shores, with established rights safeguarding fishing and navigating. Hastings, Eastbourne, Newhaven, Brighton, Worthing, Littlehampton and Bognor Regis have all expanded along the coast as the population increased. They are accessible by car and there are good beaches, which have increased the difficulties of preservation. Local Authorities are concerned with rateable values and this can influence decisions when the authority is not a wealthy one.

Badly sited bungalows and what were once temporary dwellings on the coastline should have been moved to other sites or screened from view. Eyesores of advertising, which are genuinely bogus, have short lives and can eventually be removed. Birling Gap and the Seven Sisters, which rise to over 500 feet, between Cuckmere Haven and Beachy Head are still untouched but nearby areas of coastline have been covered by buildings that have spewed forth from the towns. Stevenson's lighthouse — Belle Tout — built of Aberdeen granite in 1831 and now beheaded, is at Beachy Head as a forlorn reminder of the skill of engineers in nautical architecture. The population on the Sussex coast will increase and so will the demand for more building land on the coastline unless inland areas are used. In 1885, the Lawrence sisters founded a school for girls between Ovingdean and Brighton. The idea was ambitious and the sisters were prepared to use rooms in the town in order to have their school, Roedean, exactly where they wanted it. Today, schemes are still being approved by harassed authorities without due regard to the surrounding landscape when pressure is applied.

We have to change to meet the requirements of modern living which include increased sanitation, car parks, sports centres and recreation areas while retaining buildings of interest from the past. One solution is to encourage counter-attractions inland; recreational parks and the stimulation of interest in stately homes and areas of outstanding natural beauty, even though there are risks involved. The demand will still exist for harbourage and facilities for small boats. Difficulties also exist for siting caravans, which increase in number each year. Ports, too, are vulnerable being contact points between land and sea. Increased shipping between Sussex and Europe is a foreseeable problem which will have to be resolved. If we don't arrive at a scheme that can answer at least part of the future demands on the coast we shall be doomed to a midsummer night's dream, a bad one, " that is the true beginning of our end ".

Planners and preservationists today seem to divide the human race into two categories, those who care about the past and those who do not. This division cuts neatly through all social and racial strata. Our heritage in buildings that are part of the Sussex countryside has been squandered during the last twenty years, with the exception of castles and stately homes. The excuse, once again, has been progress but in many cases the reason has been neglect and lack of interest, or money, by the authorities concerned. There has been ample talk of polluted land, sea and air across the county but many parts have visual pollution in the form of a fine old building decaying through neglect. Hove, in particular, failed to retain Xaverian College, originally the Attree Villa in Tower Road, designed by Charles Barry in 1830. Hangleton Manor, a simple flint manor house of the 16th century, situated in Hove also, was insensitively hemmed in by a palisade of modern housing lacking pedigree. Hove Town Hall, a robust red brick and terracotta building designed by Alfred Waterhouse in 1882, was destroyed by fire, however. Even Lord Holford's attempt to save The Royal Spa, built by Dr. Struve in 1825 when Brighton's Queen's Park was a fashionable watering place, was not successful in

1971. If we ignore the loss of old buildings and do not demonstrate against visual pollution in our menaced towns, we deserve to wait in our coffins for the statutory undertakers.

Local politicians know that they gain greater prestige by building new estates than they do by restoring old houses. Too many developers hit below the green belt. They demolish a " listed " building because the fine will be paltry, or allow it to fall into such disrepair that it has to be demolished as a threat to public safety. The consolation for those who manage to save a building that is part of Sussex history — despite accusations that they are " putting the clock back " — is that they will have made a positive contribution for the future. More money is spent cleaning the offices of County and Town Halls than on preserving listed buildings, excluding churches. Cleanliness may be next to Godliness, but Heaven won't preserve our heritage. The Local Authority's response to appeals has been like a provocative smile that says little but promises much. Nobody wants to put the clock back, but those who appreciate the past and accept the future seek to accommodate changes with minimum harm to the surroundings. The Civic Trust, founded in 1956 by Duncan Sandys and financed by covenants from large Companies, has pioneered the promotion of good architecture, town planning and preservation even though, like Barbiena, they create masques and spectacles from the resources of the nobility.

The Duke of Edinburgh has said: " Every interest is partly conservationist and partly destroyer." His Royal Highness's concern for the serious ornithological study of both native and migrant birds, supporting The Wildfowl Trust, have stimulated public interest in the matter. The future success of avoiding petrified forests in Sussex and ensuring continuity of the wildlife depends on the ability of preservationists to conduct their battles by words in the ears of the influential, by liaison with land-owners, ministers, industrialists and anybody in the small inner circles of power. Individuals have to plan their own campaigns since history has shown that decisions cannot be made by Committees. It is essential to distinguish between the possible and the impossible.

Nature has endeavoured to prevent the poulation increase in species ever since there were men. The reproductive potential of the human species has enabled it to survive, greatly assisted by the development of firearms. The decline of wildlife has resulted from loss of natural habitat, often caused by bull-dozers which make " panoramic " roads through previously inaccessible areas of Sussex. Land-rovers and amphibious trucks have also left their contribution of ruts through the flora and have altered the balance of the landscape. There are dangers in drawing attention to areas of unspoiled countryside because the curious are alerted and eventually visit them. Can administrators and Government be persuaded to realise that fresh air and wild scenery are more important luxuries in Sussex than faster road links, industrial development and artificial harbours? It's like trying to push a five ton lorry uphill with a piece of rope.

The Sussex Naturalists' Trust has been fortunate in establishing reserves at Amberley Wildbrooks, Chidmere Pond, Pagham Harbour, Pagham Lagoon, Saddlescombe Chalk Pit, St. Leonards' Forest, Vert Wood and Welch's Common. Woods Mill at Henfield is also a reserve. The Wildfowl Trust will have a large sanctuary at Arundel due to the generosity of the Duke of Norfolk, who has given 60 acres of his land, half a mile from the castle, for this purpose. The sanctuary for wildfowl will be run on the lines of the ornithologist's Mecca, Slimbridge in Gloucestershire. In Arundel, the watermeadows reserve lies between Offham, Hanger Wood, the River Arun and the Mill Stream, which cover areas of outstanding natural beauty. Parts will be screened from visitors to protect the birds from disturbance and observation will be possible from hides. The marshy land, only used for rough grazing of cattle, has been saved for good use in the future.

Valleys cut through the chalk in the area set aside for The Wildfowl Trust and there are rivers for anglers — the Arun, the Adur, the Cuckmere and the Ouse — where you can watch wild duck and snipe among the reeds. The winter floods in the valleys provide long lakes for widgeon and teal. Many people are sincere in their desire to protect and preserve wildlife but I'm always slightly surprised when they can eat roast pheasant with relish. In the Arun, the longest river, you can fish for chub, pike, perch and roach upstream. Sussex has a reputation for providing gourmet's delights which include Selsey cockle, Chichester lobster, Arundel mullet, Amberley trout, Pulborough eel and Rye herring. You could buy freshly roasted linnets on sticks, if you weren't sensitive about bird life, at the beginning of the present century and be served with wheatear pie, made from the ortolans that flew over the Downs. The future of Sussex, in which there was no wildlife reserve, could find us watching a saraband for skylarks.

The National Trust has saved and protected much of the finest countryside and historic buildings, for the nation, in Great Britain. The Trust, founded in 1895, is not an official body and does not rely on Government help. Many historic buildings in Sussex have been acquired by The National Trust, the country's largest private landowner, when charity was a virtue and not an institution. Legacies and gifts have enabled the Trust to continue its vital work and threequarters of the benefactors in the 'seventies were women, of whom five-eighths were unmarried, presumably spinsters endowed with a sense of chauvinism. The houses and gardens open to the public in Sussex range from the Alfriston Clergy House, a half-timbered thatched building dating from 1350, to the castles at Bodiam and Bramber. Other properties include Lamb House at Rye, a Georgian house that was the home of Henry James from 1898 to 1916, and Bateman's which was the home of Rudyard Kipling between 1902 and 1936. The Trust owns and maintains Petworth House with its park, Nymans Gardens covering 30 acres of grounds and the Seven Sisters cliffs on the coastline.

The Countryside Commission has made sure that the public in the Sussex of tomorrow can make extensive journeys on foot and horseback, without fear of trespass, on the South Downs Way. The route runs for 80 miles between Eastbourne and the Hampshire border, mostly along the ridge of the South Downs, avoiding resorts, dormitory towns and trunk roads. The Downs, for many people, are a symbol of Sussex. They are a range of chalk hills, with steep escarpments, that have the virtues of simplicity and sturdiness. Sussex weather, with its sudden changes, is unpredictable but the outline of the Downs is clear in all conditions although the curves and folds of the landscape disappear from view when skies are cloudy or the winter light pales. The structure of the Downs is sea-made, a soft limestone of considerable depth which Sussex is fortunate to possess. The height, near Lewes, is greater than 700 feet. Sheep have grazed on the Downs for 5,000 years and are not disturbed by ramblers and pony-trekkers today. Nor is The Long Man, stretched out flat on the north face of Windover Hill above Wilmington. The white chalk figure, 226 feet high, was probably cut in the turf by a band of artistically inclined Saxons and was made a permanent feature when 700 concrete blocks secured him in 1969. He rests in pieces.

New street facades have rendered the already expressionless faces of some of the towns of Sussex even less interesting than ever. Our towns are devoted to four categories of use; living, working, recreation and communication. If high densities continue and overhead transport systems are introduced, future inhabitants will have a birds-eye view of the county. Two centuries ago, the migration to towns was sufficiently gradual to allow for the assimilation of county dwellers. In the 19th century, the increased growth of cities meant that, for certain sections of the population, life was short and unpleasant. But

the towns offered more jobs and starvation was rare. Today,
there is a parallel to the pattern of the 19th century although
there are insufficient jobs and housing for migrants to the
South and starvation does occur.

Pollution is one problem generated by a large concentration
of people in Sussex towns, with increasing sulphur dioxide, soot
and ash. Trees die suddenly, as leaves do when the sea-spray
blows inland along the coast, without explanation. The motor-
car dominates life and transport routes slice through town
centres. Even the streets are now dependant, to some degree,
on computers for traffic control, stock control in stores, records
for police and hospitals. But computers are neutral and cannot
think. I know several human beings who also answer this
description and you can recognise them as " obedients." There
will be more of them, too, since the world population will
double between now and the end of the century while building
construction must, of necessity, increase to meet the needs of
the population. Urban buildings continue to increase in
expense at the rate of $5\frac{1}{2}$ times the cost of rural construction.

The talent of earlier generations, who planned and landscaped towns in Sussex, has to be rediscovered in order that
houses and other buildings can be designed and grouped in a
considered landscape for the future. James Burton, and his
son Decimus, achieved this at St. Leonards-On-Sea, now part of
Hastings, in the 19th century. The Regency planning of
Brighton, with the rolling terraces of Kemp Town and the
elegant squares, made the resort visually exciting. The
Victorians, no less adventurous, added the piers and impressive
churches. A cosmopolitan atmosphere exists in Brighton
today but there are particularly hideous modern buildings,
with the exception of the skilful extension of The Lanes into
Brighton Square by architects Fitzroy Robinson and Partners.
Brighton's new architecture has been driven into the body of
the town like a vampire stake. Simon Jenkins has written:
" Brighton, I'm sure, is the sort of place which can survive rape
— even two times over. But for how much longer?"

The housing problem, which affects Sussex particularly as
people overspill from London or move southwards from the
Midlands, is due to a lack of building land. Houses that are
being built are offered for sale at high prices, Council housing
is limited and rents for flats are among the highest in the
country. The younger generation, who want to spend their
future in the county, have to face a situation where the limited
accommodation goes mainly to retired, middle-aged or business
people. Those fortunate individuals who have managed to
move into Sussex have been far-sighted in obtaining key jobs

with sufficient money to buy their own home. There are towns
in other parts of the country where property prices are lower
but the appeal of Sussex, a rich area of green and pleasant land,
is like a love affair for the bewitched and one which cannot
always be consummated.

It may be foolish to have hope for the human state but hope
is necessary in difficult circumstances. When new horizons
appear they encourage optimism. The University of Sussex is
one source of hope for the future. In 1958, it was the second
university in England after Keele and work on the buildings
started in 1960 at Falmer, a true village in one of the small
valleys north of the road between Lewes and Brighton. The
architect, Sir Basil Spence, achieved the difficult task of
designing a layout that had to grow and yet have unity. He
has said that the ruin of the Colosseum was the spiritual source
and the result was an asymmetrical grouping of buildings that
were romantically landscaped to accentuate the natural beauty
of the surroundings. The Royal Charter was received in 1961
and the Gardner Arts Centre, which unites the town of
Brighton with the gown of Falmer, was an imaginative addition
to the University in the late 'sixties. Professor Asa Briggs has
championed a liberal approach to learning at the University of
Sussex with these words: "Society needs specialists but it
does not want narrow specialists. It depends upon skills, but
it also requires the ability to make wise judgements. Natural
survival, human survival, cannot be guaranteed by experts
alone. Separated teams of experts, indeed, could lead to
disaster."

Words, like those, of outward looking men are needed to arouse people who are too concerned with themselves and indifferent to the world outside. If we don't recognise the symbols that are a mark of character in Sussex then we are not likely to hear the warning drums that are a continual reminder of future danger on the coast, in the countryside and in the towns. The essential and unique character of the county should be retained and what perceptive people achieve today, with that as their objective, will benefit others tomorrow. Conviction is not easy to acquire. Tolerance, contentment and simple living are equally elusive in some lives. There's no future in them, you may think. But, like an air cushion, they smooth out the bumps in life and remain as clear in outline as the Sussex Downs.

INDEX